Machine Learning For Beginners Guide Algorithms:

Supervised & Unsupervised Learning Decision Tree & Random Forest Introduction

Introduction:

Chapter 1: About Machine Learning

What is Machine Learning?

History:

Chapter 2: Machine Learning Basics

Differences between Traditional Programming and Machine Learning

Elements of Machine Learning

Types and Kinds of Machine Learning

Machine Learning in Practice

Learning models

Sample applications of machine learning

Chapter 3: Machine Learning: Algorithms

Ensemble Learning Method

Supervised Learning

Unsupervised Learning

Semi-Supervised Learning

Algorithms Grouped By Similarity

Chapter 4: Decision Tree and Random Forests: Part One

What is a Decision Tree? How exactly does it work?

Decision Tree, Algorithms

Types of Decision Trees

Terminology and Jargon related to Decision Trees

Advantages

Disadvantages

Regression Trees vs. Classification Trees

Where does the tree get split?

Gini Index

Chi-Square

Information Gain, Decision Tree

Reduction in Variance

Chapter 5: Decision Trees: Part 2

Tree Pruning

Linear models or tree based models?

Ensemble methods:

What is Bagging? How does it work?

Chapter 6: Decision Trees: Part Three (Random Forests)

Workings of Random Forest:

Advantages of Random Forest

Disadvantages of Random Forest

What is Boosting? How does it work?

By utilizing average or weighted average

How do we choose a different distribution for each round?

GBM or XGBoost: Which is more powerful?

How to work with GBM in R and Python?

Chapter 7: Deep Learning

The difference between Machine Learning, Deep Learning, and AI:

Chapter 8: Digital Neural Network and Computer Science

Applications of ANN

Advantages of ANN

Risks associated with ANN

Types of Artificial Neural Networks

Conclusion

© **Healthy Pragmatic Solutions Inc. Copyright 2017 - All rights reserved.**

The contents of this book may not be reproduced, duplicated or transmitted without direct written permission from the author.

Under no circumstances will any legal responsibility or blame be held against the publisher for any reparation, damages, or monetary loss due to the information herein, either directly or indirectly.

Legal Notice:

You cannot amend, distribute, sell, use, quote or paraphrase any part or the content within this book without the consent of the author.

Disclaimer Notice:

Please note the information contained within this document is for educational purposes only. No warranties of any kind are expressed or implied. Readers acknowledge that the author is not engaging in the rendering of legal, financial, medical or professional advice. Please consult a licensed professional before attempting any techniques outlined in this book.

By reading this document, the reader agrees that under no circumstances are is the author responsible for any losses, direct or indirect, which are incurred as a result of the use of information contained within this document, including, but not limited to, —errors, omissions, or inaccuracies

Introduction

I want to thank you for choosing this book, *'Machine learning for beginners - Algorithms, Decision Tree & Random Forest Introduction.'*

By choosing this book, you have made the right decision, as you will learn many new, innovative and exciting things about the world of technology and computers. It will help you learn the basics of AI and machine learning in a simple, entertaining and informative way.

Currently one of the most talked about topics in the world of technology, machine learning is a promising concept. But along with the promises and benefits, it is also often associated with controversies and debates.

People who are not aware of the nature and advantages of machine learning or have received their information from untrustworthy sources often look down on machine learning and are scared of it as well. However, all the strange and bizarre things that you have heard about machine learning are probably just myths and false apprehensions.

This book will try to do away with such apprehensions by showing how machine learning is perhaps the best thing that could happen to the world of technology right now. You will get answers to all your questions about machine learning and more. So, rather than making assumptions, you will learn and understand what machine learning is all about and make your own decisions.

So let's read on.

Chapter 1: About Machine Learning

One of the best features of today's era of technology is its flexibility and adaptableness. A new scientific innovation comes out almost every day. This ever-changing nature of scientific and technological world changes the trajectory of the world every day. Things that were considered dreams and fiction once are now rapidly turning into reality. Human beings are slowly but steadily trying to defeat nature at its own game. However, one field remains to be conquered. We still have not managed to conquer the world of machine learning or AI. However, it has become a buzzword now, and the whole of the world is talking about it. Not everyone is excited about it though. Most people are worried or scared of it. However, there is no need to be afraid of machine learning or AI, as it will help humanity to achieve things that we cannot even currently imagine.

What is Machine Learning?

If you check the search results for the most popular keywords of 2016, you will find that machine learning and AI are leading the figures by a large margin. This steady rise in the fame of machine learning is because of its rising use in our daily lives. It is nowadays being used in various devices and machines as well as gadgets. However, the general population is still are wary of it. So, to do away with such myths, let us have a look at the brief history of machine learning.

As per the 1959 definition of Arthur Samuel, machine learning can be defined as a process of inputting data to the computer systems in a way that the computer will learn the ability to process and perform the activity in the future without being explicitly programmed or being fed with similar or extra data. What this means in simple words is that it will allow computers to develop a 'mind' of their own and allow them to "think." Sounds scary but it isn't.

If computers are provided with the ability to think, they become smarter and thus easier to use. Their functionality will increase by a large margin, and they become an integral asset for humanity. Machine learning can be used in almost all the fields of epistemology. Right now, it is being used in areas such as cheminformatics, computational anatomy, gaming, adaptive websites, natural language processing, robot movement and locomotion, medical diagnosis, sequence mining, behavior analysis, linguistics, translation, fraud detection, etc. The list goes on.

History:

The history of machine learning can be traced to the birth of another related field- AI or artificial intelligence. It is safe to say that both of these fields were born at the same time and then got separated over time. Many scientists studying AI in the beginning slowly shifted towards studying machine learning academically. They started using probabilistic reasoning etc. Around the '90s the two fields, AI and machine learning, were officially separated, and now both of them are studied individually. In the following chapters, you will learn the basics of machine learning and how it can be used in day-to-day life. You will also learn about the careers that are available in this field as well as certain advanced topics for the experts.

Chapter 2: Machine Learning Basics

What is it that has made machine learning a buzzword in today's era? The simplest answer to the above question would be its unique, feature-rich nature that can change the future of humanity forever. In the words of Bill Gates:

"A breakthrough in machine learning would be worth ten Microsofts."

What the above statement roughly means is that scientists and computer experts all over are desperately looking for a breakthrough in machine learning and are looking for a way to make it more accessible, useful and trustworthy. However, such programs are still going, and we still haven't found a way to devise a machine that could think.

In machine learning, computers learn to program themselves. If programming is considered to be automation and an automatic process, then machine learning is the automation of this automatic process, thus making a double automatic process.

Machine learning can make programming more scalable and can help us to produce better results in shorter durations. To prove this, let us see the following comparison:

Differences between Traditional Programming and Machine Learning

Traditional Programming:

The data is fed to the computer, and a program is run. This program then, using the supplied data, presents output.

Machine Learning:

Pre-solved data and the resulting output are fed to the computer. These two inputs are used to create a program. This program then can do the job of traditional programming.

Thus, machine learning can be explained by using the metaphors of agriculture. Algorithms are, in a way seeds while data is nutrients. You are the farmer while the program that grows out of the data is your crop.

Elements of Machine Learning

As machine learning is a complicated and convoluted field, it's hard to understand its basics. It is also an ever-growing field. Hence it is possible to see new development in the area almost every day. For instance, it is believed that every year more than a few hundred, new algorithms are developed all over the world. This brings the number of overall machine learning algorithms to a sum that is larger than ten thousand. Even though a lot of variety is seen in the algorithms of machine learning, all of them are based on three basic concepts that are as follows.

Representation:

This concept deals with the representation of knowledge. It deals with how the knowledge can be represented, what is necessary to represent the knowledge etc. Some examples of representation include sets of rules, including decision trees, support vector machines, instances, neural networks, graphical models, model ensembles, etc. Some of these will be discussed in the book later.

Evaluation:

This is the second most important concept of algorithms. It is the way used to evaluate the hypotheses, also known as the candidate program. Some examples are accuracy, prediction and recall, squared error, likelihood, posterior probability, cost, margin, entropy k-L divergence and others.

Optimization:

This is the third and last concept of algorithms. It is the method in which the hypothesis or the candidate program is created. It is also known as the search process. Examples include combinatorial optimization, convex optimization and constrained optimization.

Making various combinations of the above components creates all machine-learning algorithms, and thus they are the basis of machine learning.

Types and Kinds of Machine Learning

As said earlier, machine learning is complex and vast field hence it can be divided into many sections and classes. However, on a superficial level, it can be split into four parts, and they are as follows:

1. Supervised Learning
2. Unsupervised Learning
3. Semi-supervised Learning
4. Reinforcement Learning

Supervised learning:

Supervised Learning is also known as inductive learning in the technological circles. It is considered to be the most advanced and mature of all the forms of learning. This is why it is the most studied as well as most used learning as well. It is easy to used Learning type as it is much easier to learn under supervision than without supervision. In Inductive Learning, we are presented with an example of a function in the form of data (x), and the output of the function is (f(x)). The mission of inductive learning here is to understand and learn the function for the new data (x).

In this learning, the program is 'trained' with the help of some already defined set of 'examples.' This training helps the program to learn the ability to formulate a new and accurate result using the newly fed data with ease and without any interference.

Supervised learning is the most used and most favorite of all forms of learning, this chapter as well as this book will try to focus on it. Other types will be discussed briefly.

In most of the supervised learning applications, the final mission is to create a proper and well-set predictor function h(x). It is also known as the hypothesis. The 'learning' contains many mathematical algorithms that are necessary to optimize the function. When it is optimized, it can correctly predict the value of h(x) if data X is fed to the computer related to a particular domain. For instance, if the data being fed is the square footage of agricultural land, the program should be able to return the estimated price for the piece of land.

However, it is seen that x always represents more than one data point. For instance, if we are to continue the above example, then the program may take the number of wells (x_2), number of trees (x_3), number of greenhouses (x_4), number of electric poles (x_5), number compost holes (x6) and many other variables along with the first one that is the square footage of the land (x1). Then the determination of the correct input is the input that will come out with the correct result. This is one of the major parts of machine learning design. However, as the topic might get too complex and complicated, this example will only assume a single input value.

Example

Let us assume that the program or predictor is using this form:

H (x) = θ0 + θ1x

Here θ0 and θ1 are constants. The mission here is to find the perfect values for the above two constants to create and make our predictor work properly.

To optimize the predictor h (x), training examples are used. In each of these examples a value of x train is added and corresponding to this value an output value- y is already known. For instance, the difference between the known i.e. correct value y, and the predicted value h (x train) is found. When enough training examples are fed, the differences can be studied and checked to determine and measure our faults of h (x). Using our findings, we can change and manipulate the h (x) by manipulating the values of θ_0 and θ_1 to make it more accurate. This process then is repeated until the best values of θ_0 and θ_1 are found. This is how the predictor is trained. This trained predictor can now read real life data and predict perfectly to almost perfect results.

Unsupervised learning:

The data that is fed to the system i.e. the training data does not include any desired output. Thus, the data that is to be fed is without output. It is difficult to understand and proclaim that whether this is good and recommended method of learning or not. Examples include clustering etc.

Semi-supervised learning:

This is a mixture of both the above kinds of learning where training data contains some but not all desired outputs.

Reinforcement learning:

Considered to be the most ambitious of all the types of learning. Here rewards are given from a sequence of actions. AI often prefers this.

Machine Learning in Practice

Although an important part of the overall machine learning process, machine algorithms are a tiny part of the complete process. In reality, the process is much more complicated. An example is as follows:

Start Loop

Here the domain is to be understood. The current data on hand, available knowledge and goals are analyzed. This often includes communicating with the domain experts. The goals are often unclear, and you have to attempt and try many things before implementing anything.

Data integration, selection, cleaning and pre-processing

This is the most time-consuming part in the overall process. It takes almost half or more than half of the overall required processing time. Procuring high-quality data is critical. However, the quality and quantity of data are often reversely proportional as the more the data, the more it will be dirty. Sorting out good and usable data from the rest is why this process takes a very long time.

Learning models

This part, though being the most mature part of the process, is also the most fun part of it. General tools are used for this.

Interpreting results

In many cases, it is not necessary to understand how the model works, the only focus being the results. Often human experts can challenge you on this.

Consolidating and deploying discovered knowledge.

Though many projects succeed in the lab and are remarkable, yet the chances of them being used in real life are quite rare. Most of the projects are discarded and not used in real life at all.

End Loop

There is an end cycle at the end, and it is not a one-shot process. It is necessary to run the loop until a desired and usable result is achieved. The data can also change midway, affecting the overall process, as you need a new loop to replace the earlier one.

Sample applications of machine learning

This is a small list of fields in which machine learning can be applied to achieve great results:

- Web search: It can rank web pages and search entries according to your previous clicks and likes and will prominently show new, similar results.
- Computational biology: Can rationally create drugs in the system or computer using old and past experiments.
- Finance: Can evaluate how much risk is present on a credit card. Can also be used to send tailored offers according to the likings of a customer. Can also help you in choosing where to invest money.
- E-commerce: Identifying a transaction's nature, whether it is a true and correct transaction or whether it is a fraudulent one. It can also help you in predicting the number of customers.
- Space exploration: Can help with radio astronomy and space probes.
- Robotics: Can help to create self-driving cars and autonomous robots. Can contribute to building robots that can

handle uncertain situations and new environments.
- Information extraction: Can extract information from databases on the web.
- Social networks: Can help you get data on preferences and relationships.
- Debugging: Can be used for debugging.

Chapter 3: Machine Learning: Algorithms

While discussing the basics of machine learning in the last chapter, we talked briefly about machine learning in algorithms. Let us take a deeper look at the algorithms, their types, the most popular ones and everything else about them in this chapter.

As said in the last chapter, the sheer number of algorithms that are available can overwhelm any beginner to machine learning. Therefore, it is necessary to categorize them in two large sections for our convenience.

There are two ways of classifying algorithms; the first one is categorizing them by learning style while the second is the grouping of algorithms by the similarity of function or form. Both of these techniques or methods of categorizing are useful, however, let us algorithms by similarity category and check out its nuances.

Ensemble Learning Method

There are a variety of ways in which an algorithm can base a problem that relies on the interactions that take place with the experience or environment or any other form of input data.

It is highly popular in artificial intelligence as well as machine learning textbooks to consider the learning styles of an algorithm first followed by everything else later.

An algorithm can have only a few relevant learning models or learning styles. These will be explained in the sections below.

The categorization, or to use the scientific term, taxonomy/organization of machine learning algorithms is highly desirable as it makes you think of the roles of input data as well as the model preparation process. You can then choose one that is the best for your problem to get the best result.

Although covered briefly in the first chapter, these are the three different but basic learning styles:

Supervised Learning

In this, the input data is known as training data. It features a known result or a label, for instance, spam/not-spam or stock price, etc. A proper prediction model is constructed using the training process. It is needed to make predictions, and these predictions get corrected if they are wrong. The training process continues to repeat itself until perfection, or the desired level of accuracy is achieved.

Examples: Logistic Regression and the Back Propagation Neural Network.

Unsupervised Learning

The data under this category does not have a known output or result neither does it have a label.

The prediction model is constructed by guessing the number of structures present in the input data, often to take out general rules.

Example problems include dimensionality reduction, clustering, and association rule learning.

Example algorithms include various algorithms such as the Apriori algorithm and k-Means.

Semi-Supervised Learning

In this, the input data has no solid form and is a jumbled a mixture of labeled as well as unlabeled examples.

The model needs to learn the structures that are necessary to not only organize the data but make predictions as well.

Example problems include classification and regression.

Example algorithms are extensions.

Algorithms Grouped By Similarity

As said earlier, algorithms can be classified on various bases. They are often classified by the similarities that are seen in their functioning. For instance, neural network inspired methods and tree-based methods.

It is considered to be one of the best ways of grouping algorithms and is one of the most used methods. However, it is not perfect as many algorithms exist that cannot be classified in watertight compartments. For instance, the Learning Vector Quantization is a method that is an instance-based method and a neural network inspired method. Thus, it is not possible to classify the algorithms on a deeper level with just two criteria. Hence, people often use a nested approach while classifying machine learning algorithms.

There are many algorithms and groups of algorithms. Some of the major and frequently used are listed below.

Regression Algorithms

These deal with the modeling of the relationship among the variables. This relationship is iteratively refined with the help of a measure of error in the predictions or probability that is achieved by the model. They often work on the base of statistics and are now used in statistical machine learning. People find this slightly confusing as regression can be used to refer to the class of the problem as well as the class of the algorithm itself, however, basically, regression is said to be a process.

Some of the highly popular regression algorithms include:

- Ordinary Least Squares Regression (OLSR)
- Linear Regression
- Logistic Regression

- Stepwise Regression
- Multivariate Adaptive Regression Splines (MARS)
- Locally Estimated Scatterplot Smoothing (LOESS)

Instance-based Algorithms

Instance-based learning is a model that is a decision problem with examples of training data. These are considered to be important or necessary for the model. These methods often build up a database of example data. This is then compared with the new data to the database with the help of similarity measure. This is done to locate the best match and throw out a prediction. This is the reason why instance-based methods are often known as winner-take-all methods as well as memory-based learning. The primary focus in this method is the representation of the stored instances as well as the similarity measures used between them.

Following are the highly instance-based algorithms:

- K-Nearest Neighbor (kNN)
- Learning Vector Quantization (LVQ)
- Self-Organizing Map (SOM)
- Locally Weighted Learning (LWL)

Regularization Algorithms

These serve as an extension or a secondary method to another method such as regression method. They are used to punish the models by their complicatedness and favor the simpler models that are good at generalizing.

Highly used regularization algorithms are:

- Ridge Regression
- Least Absolute Shrinkage and Selection Operator (LASSO)
- Elastic Net
- Least-Angle Regression (LARS)

Decision Tree Algorithms

Decision tree methods manufacture a model of decisions that have been made based on the real values of attributes in the available data. A fork is formed in the decision tree until a prediction is made for the provided record. They are often trained for the classification of data as well as regression problems. They are quite fast as well as accurate, making them highly popular and a favorite in the world of machine learning.

Standard decision tree algorithms are as follows:

- Classification and Regression Tree (CART)
- Iterative Dichotomiser 3 (ID3)
- C4.5 and C5.0 (different versions of a robust approach)
- Chi-squared Automatic Interaction Detection (CHAID)
- Decision Stump

- M5
- Conditional Decision Trees

Bayesian Algorithms

These methods are known as Bayesian methods as they explicitly apply Bayes' Theorem for various problems that include classification and regression.

The most common Bayesian algorithms are:

- Naive Bayes
- Gaussian Naive Bayes
- Multinomial Naive Bayes
- Averaged One-Dependence Estimators (AODE)
- Bayesian Belief Network (BBN)
- Bayesian Network (BN)

Clustering Algorithms

These are like regression as they describe the class of problem as well as the class of methods. Different modeling approaches organize them, for instance, centroid-based and hierarchal. All of these use the inbuilt structures in the data for a better organization of the data into small groups of maximum commonality.

Following are the highly popular clustering algorithms:

- K-Means
- K-Medians
- Expectation Maximization (EM)
- Hierarchical Clustering

Association Rule Learning Algorithms

It identifies the rules that evaluate the relationships between data and variables. These rules can find many commercially useful and relevant associations in massive and multidimensional data sets. These can be used with organizations.

Some examples include:

- Apriori algorithm
- Eclat algorithm

Artificial Neural Network Algorithms

These are networks that have been modeled and inspired by the functioning and structures of the biological nerves. They are often used for classification problems as well as regression, but it may encompass various other things, as it is a huge field with various epistemological fields and sides.

Highly popular artificial neural network algorithms include:

- Perceptron
- Back-Propagation
- Hopfield Network
- Radial Basis Function Network (RBFN)
- Deep Learning Algorithms

Deep Learning Algorithms

These are modern and highly up to date artificial neural networks that can use cheap and abundant computation. You will find more about these in the following chapters. These concern with the construction of large as well as highly complex networks of neurons.

Some of the most popular deep learning algorithms include:

- Deep Boltzmann Machine (DBM)
- Deep Belief Networks (DBN)
- Convolutional Neural Network (CNN)
- Stacked Auto-Encoders
- Dimensionality Reduction Algorithms

Dimensional Reduction Algorithms

These are like clustering methods, and they try to find and use the inbuilt structure of the data. In these cases, this is done in an unsupervised manner.

This can be useful to visualize dimensional data or to simplify data that can then be used in a supervised learning method.

Ensemble Algorithms

These models are made of various weaker models that have been trained independently to work on specific tasks. The predictions of all these models are then combined to form an ensemble prediction. A lot of effort is put into the types of weak learners as well as how they can be combined. It is supposed to be a highly powerful technique.

Chapter 4: Decision Tree and Random Forests: Part One

This and the following two chapters will deal with the primary subject matter of this books i.e. decision trees and random forests. As decision trees and random forests is a vast field, it has been broken down into three chapters for the ease of the reader, so that even if the reader is a beginner or an amateur, they would be able to follow the information in the book. Let us now begin with the basics of decision trees.

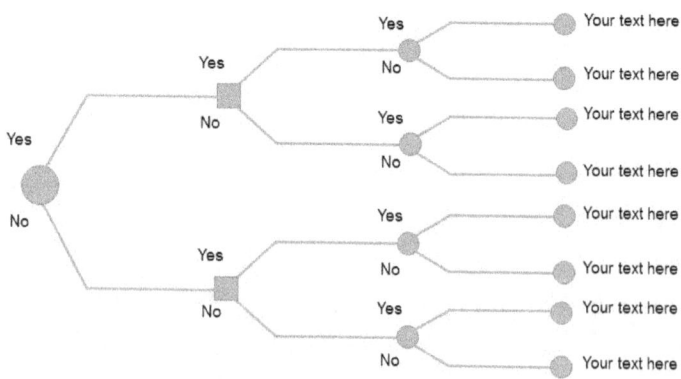

What is a Decision Tree? How exactly does it work?

Before beginning any topic, it is necessary to understand the basics of it and what it entitles. Thus, this section will deal with general information regarding Decision Trees.

In simple language a Decision Tree can be defined as a kind or type of learning algorithm that is supervised and has a pre-defined target variable that is commonly used in classification problems. Classification problems are a forte of Decision Trees as they fit perfectly with classification problems.

Decision trees can be used in both continuous input output variables as well as categorical output variables. In this method, the sample is split into two or more homogeneous sets by most significant splitter or differentiator in input variables.

Example:

Let's take a look at a sample of 30 children with three different variables viz. Gender (M or F), Town (A or B) and Weight (50 to 60 kg). 15 of these 30 play piano in their free time. Now, the condition is that I want to create a model that will predict who plays piano in their free time.

For this problem, it is necessary to differentiate the children and add them in categories such as children who play the piano. This should be based on highly significant input variable in between all the three.

In such a case a decision tree can help a lot as it differentiates and categorizes children using all the all the three variables and will form the most homogenous groups of students that will be heterogeneous to each other.

Decision Tree, Algorithms

Decision trees, as mentioned above finds and identifies the most significant variable as well as its value. This finds the best homogeneous set of data. However, the question that comes out of this is how does it do this, i.e. how does it identify the variable as well as the split. The decision tree uses a variety of algorithms to perform this action. These algorithms will be discussed in the next few sections of this chapter.

Types of Decision Trees

The categorization of the decision tree can be based on the kind of target variable that is available. It is found that it can be of two types:

Categorical Variable Decision Tree:

A Decision Tree that has categorical target variable is known as a categorical variable decision tree. For instance: If we are to continue the above example. The target variable in it will be "Children play piano or not." i.e. YES or NO.

Continuous Variable Decision Tree:

This is the second type of decision tree. If the tree has an ongoing target variable, it is known as Continuous Variable Decision Tree.

Example: Instead of continuing the above example, let us try something different. Let's assume that a person will pay his tax to the tax department (Yes/No). Here it is seen that the income of the individual is the important variable. However, the tax company may or may not have the details of the person. Now, as we already are aware of the importance of the variable, a decision tree can be constructed to predict the income using variables like the product, occupation, etc. In such a case the predictions are happening for a continuous variable.

Terminology and Jargon related to Decision Trees

As machine learning is a complicated and complex topic, it has its language that is full of jargon. Similarly, the field of Decision Tree too has its jargon that is often full of tree metaphors. Let us have a look at the most important idioms.

- Root Node: It stands for the total sample or population. It is then further divided into two or more homogeneous sets.
- Splitting: This is the process that is used to classify nodes into two or more sub-nodes.

- Decision Node: The further division of sub-nodes into more sub-nodes is also known as splitting. However, the node created in this process is known as a decision node.
- Leaf/ Terminal Node: The Nodes that cannot be split are known as Leaf or Terminal node.
- Pruning: Continuing the metaphors of tree and plants, the process in which the subnodes of a decision node are removed, is known as pruning. It is thus an anti-splitting process.
- Branch / Sub-Tree: As the name suggests, the sub-section of a complete tree is known as a sub-tree or branch.
- Parent and Child Node: In the division of the nodes, the node that gets divided is referred as a parent node, while the nodes that are formed due to this division, i.e. the sub-nodes are known as child nodes.

These are the most commonly used jargons in the Decision Tree terminology. Now let us have a look at the advantages and disadvantages of the algorithm.

There exists no perfect machine-learning algorithm, and all algorithms have one problem or the other. Hence, instead of criticizing an algorithm, it is necessary to study its advantages and disadvantages and use it according to your requirements and needs. Below you will find the pros and cons of decision tree algorithm discussed in brief.

Advantages

Easy to understand:

Even for the people who do not have an analytical background, decision tree algorithm is very easy to comprehend. A user does not need to have any statistical knowledge or information to study, read and interpret the trees. Users can easily read the data in decision trees, as the graphical representation is highly intuitive and user-friendly.

Useful in Data exploration:

It is believed that decision tree, if not the fastest, then definitely one of the fastest method of identification of the most significant variable as well as the relation between two or more than two variables. A decision tree can help users to create new variables as well as features. These new features will have more strength for predicting the target variable. It is also usable in the data exploration stage. For instance, let's say the user is working on a project where the data is available in the form of multiple variables. Here the decision tree will work and predict the most significant variable with ease.

Less data cleaning required:

As said in the first chapter, in machine learning, a user has to spend most of their time in data cleaning and separating the good data from the bad data. However, in the case of the decision tree, this process is considerably easy and does not take a lot of time. It remains uninfluenced by the missing values as well as outliers, and thus the cleaning process becomes straightforward.

The data type is not a constraint:
Decision tree is a versatile algorithm, and it can handle categorical as well as numerical data variables with ease.

Non-Parametric Method:
A nonparametric method means a method that has no assumptions regarding classifier structures or spatial distribution. A decision tree is a non-parametric method.

Disadvantages

Over fitting:
Decision tree models have many difficulties out of which over fitting is the most common and practical. However, this problem can be solved with using constraints on model parameters as

well as pruning. An example is discussed in the following section.

Not fit for continuous variables:
Although it can work with continuous variables, it is not at all suitable for it. Decision tree starts losing information when it starts categorizing variables in more and more categories.

Regression Trees vs. Classification Trees

The last stage in a decision tree is the terminal nodes that are also known as the leaves. What this means is that the decision trees are normally constructed upside down, where the leaves are at the bottom while the roots are at the top.

The above-mentioned trees, both work in similar or almost similar ways, however there exist some minor differences that are quite important. Let us go through them one by one.

When the dependent variable is continuous, the regression trees are used whereas when the dependent variable is categorical; the classification trees are used.

The value gained by the terminal nodes in the sample data is the mean of response observed in the case of a regression tree. Therefore, in the case of data observation, its prediction is the mean value.

Whereas, the class gained by the terminal node in the sample data is the mode of observation in the case of the classification tree. Therefore, if some unseen data comes under that region the prediction that takes place the mode value.

Both the types of trees separate the predictor space in different, non-overlapping spaces. They are in a way, high- dimensional boxes.

Both trees use a top-down greedy method. This approach is known as recursive binary splitting. It is a top-down method as it starts from the top of the tree, where the observations are present in a single region and then divides the predictor space into two new branches down the tree. It is said to be 'greedy' as, the algorithm that looks for a best available variable in only the current split. It does not concern about the future splits that lead to a superior tree. The splitting or dividing process goes on until the stopping criterion defined by the user is achieved. For instance: the user can order the algorithm to stop as soon as the number of observations in each node goes below than 50.

In such cases, the dividing process or the splitting process gives an output of fully constructed or grown trees until the criterion is reached. However, it is most likely that the data will over-fit the tree. This leads to a bad accuracy in the form of unseen data. Due to this, pruning is necessary. It is normally used for solving the problem of over-fitting. More on this in the next section!

Where does the tree get split?

Where should the tree get split is an important question that all the users ask. This decision often affects the trees' accuracy by a large margin. However, the criteria that are used to make this decision are different in the case of classification and regression trees.

Multiple algorithms are used by the decision trees to make decisions where to split and how much to split. There is an increase in the homogeneity when the sub-nodes are created. This means that the purity of the nodes is enhanced when the target variable increases.

The selection of algorithm is also based on the kind of target variables. The four, most commonly used algorithms in such decision trees are:

Gini Index

In Gini Index, if two items are selected from a population, randomly, then they need to be of the same class. The probability for this will be one of the population will be pure.

- It will work with the categorical target variable such as "Success" or "Failure."
- It can only do Binary splits.
- The more the value of Gini, the more the value of homogeneity.
- Gini method is used to do binary splits by the CART (Classification and Regression Tree).

Let us look at the steps that can be used to calculate by Gini for a split:

The following formula is used to calculate the Gini for the subnodes

Sum of square of probability for success and failure i.e. (p^2+q^2)

Now calculate the Gini for the division for weighted Gini of each node of the created split.

For instance: In our first example, where we need to segregate the children on the basis of target variable i.e. playing piano or not.

Decision Tree, Algorithm, Gini IndexSplit on Gender:

Calculate, Gini for sub-node Female = (0.2)*(0.2) + (0.8)*(0.8) =0.68

Gini for sub-node Male = (0.65)*(0.65) + (0.35)*(0.35) =0.55

Calculate weighted Gini for Split Gender = (10/30)*0.68 + (20/30)*0.55 = 0.59

Similar for Split on Class:

Gini for sub-node Class IX = (0.43)*(0.43) + (0.57)*(0.57) =0.51

Gini for sub-node Class X = (0.56)*(0.56) + (0.44)*(0.44) =0.51

Calculate weighted Gini for Split Class = (14/30)*0.51 + (16/30)*0.51 = 0.51

Above, you can see that Gini score for Split on Gender is higher than Split on Class, hence, the node split will take place on Gender.

Chi-Square

This algorithm is used to find the statistical significance of the differences between the parent node and the sub-node. We can calculate it by the sum of all the squares of all the differences between the expected frequencies of target variable and observed frequencies of the target variable.

Categorical target variable "Success" or "Failure" are used.

It can perform two or more than two splits.

The more the value of Chi-Square the higher is the value of the statistical significance of differences between the parent node and the sub-node.

The following formula is used to calculate the Chi-Square of each node:

Chi-square = ((Actual − Expected)^2 / Expected)^1/2

The formula forms a tree that is known as CHAID (Chi-square Automatic Interaction Detector)

Necessary steps to undertake to calculate Chi-square for a split:

The Chi-square for an individual node is to be calculated by calculating the deviation for 'Success' as well as 'Failure' both.

The resultant Chi-square are then added and summed to calculate the ultimate Chi-square.

Information Gain, Decision Tree

Now it is possible to construct a conclusion that a low amount of impure nodes need less information to describe them. This information theory is used to measure and define the degree of disorganization in a system. This is known as Entropy. For instance, if a sample is 100% homogeneous then the entropy level is zero, however, if the sample is divided equally then the entropy level is 1 or one.

The lesser the entropy, the better it is.

How to calculate entropy for a split:

Calculate and formulate the entropy of parent node.

Formulate the entropy of each separate node in the split and then calculate the average weighted of all the other nodes that are present in the split.

Reduction in Variance

Until now we have seen the algorithms for target variables. When the variance is reduced, it is an algorithm that can be used in continuous target variables. This algorithm utilizes standard formula of variance that can be used to choose the best split.

How to calculate Variance:

Formulate the variance for each node.

Formulate the variance for every split as a weighted average of every node variance.

Till now we have seen the basics of decision trees as well as the basics of decision-making process that chooses the best splits for a tree model. This tree can be used and applied to both classification problems and regression problems.

How to avoid over-fitting in trees and what are the main parameters in tree modeling?

Over-fitting is one of the major problems that researchers face when constructing decision trees. If a limit does not exist in a decision tree, then it presents you 100% accuracy. However, in the worse case scenario, it will construct one leaf for every observation. Thus, it becomes extremely important to avoid over-fitting while constructing a decision tree. This can be done using the following two methods:

- Setting constraints on tree size
- Tree pruning

Let us discuss the first one in brief.

How to set Constraints on Tree Size

This can be performed using a variety of parameters that can be used to define a tree.

These parameters are explained below. These are irrespective of the tool used. These parameters are available in R as well as Python.

- Minimum Samples for a node split.
- It can define a number of observations that are needed for a required node for splitting.
- It is also used to limit over-fitting. A large number of values can prevent learning relations.

- A large number of values can also lead to under-fitting.
- It can define the minimum sample for a leaf.
- It can be used to control over-fitting.
- Lower values are appreciated for the imbalanced class problems, as the regions in which minority class turns out to be majority class are minuscule.

Maximum Depth of Tree:

- This can be used to check the depth of a tree.
- It is used to control over-fitting.
- It needs to be tuned using CV.
- It has a large number of terminal nodes.

Chapter 5: Decision Trees: Part 2

In this chapter certain topics such as tree pruning, etc. will be handled.

Tree Pruning

As mentioned in the last chapter, the method of setting a constraint is considered to be a greedy-approach, and thus, it is not recommended. What this means is that the method will just check for the best split and more on forward until one of the many given stopping conditions are achieved. For, instance if we are to use the metaphors of driving then:

Let us assume that there are two lanes.

In lane one, cars are moving at 90km/h.

In lane two, trucks are moving at 40km/h.

You are driving a red car, and now you have two options. You can either take a left turn and overtake the two cars that are driving in front of you, as soon as possible, or continue to be in your lane.

Let us now go through these choices one by one. In the choice number one, you will take over the cars immediately and then move into a lane where the trucks are driving. Now you will have to drive in the lane with the trucks at the speed of 40km/h until a spot opens up in the old lane. Meanwhile, the cars in the original lane, which were behind you, have moved on and gone ahead of you. Your choice would be the best choice if your mission were to cover the most distance in around 20 seconds. However, in the latter choice, you will continue with your speed, cross the trucks and then get a chance to take over and go ahead.

This is the difference between pruning and normal decision tree. A decision tree that has constraints will not be able to see the 'truck' or the obstruction in front of it and will try to take a greedy approach. However, if pruning is used, the method will take a few steps back and will get a chance to think upon the condition before acting on it.

This means that pruning is better than the other option. So how to use it?

For utilizing pruning, it is necessary to make decision tree with a large depth.

Then we need to begin at the bottom and then slowly and gradually start cutting off the leaves that are presenting negative results as compared from the top.

For instance, if a split is giving a result of -10 i.e. the loss of 10, then in the subsequent split should give us a gain of 20.

A simple decision tree will halt its working at step one, however, after pruning, we will begin to see the overall gain rising to +10 all the while keeping both the leaves.

Linear models or tree based models?

The use of the algorithm is dependent on the type of problem that you are trying to solve. Let us have a look at some factors that you need to consider and that can help you decide the algorithm that is to be used when solving a problem:

If the relationship between independent and dependent variable is approximated using a linear model, the linear regression will outperform the model.

If there exists a high nonlinearity as well as the complex relationship between the independent & dependent variables, a tree model will serve better than a regular method.

A decision table is a much easy to understand and explain model as compared to a linear model.

Ensemble methods:

The dictionary meaning of the word ensemble is a group. Thus, ensemble methods are made of a group of predictive models that can gain better stability and accuracy. They are also known to boost the tree-based models.

Like all other models that we have seen by now, a decision tree based model too has certain problems. These problems include bias and variance. Here bias stands for the difference between the average values that predicted than the actual values. Variance refers to the variety of the predictions of models at the same point if the samples are taken from one same population.

When the complexity of the model is increased, it is possible to see the reduction in the prediction error thanks to lower bias in the model. However, when you gradually continue to build a more complicated model you can over-fit your model, and thus your model may suffer from the high variance.

A strong and highly powerful model should be able to maintain a proper balance between the above-mentioned types of errors. This is also known as the trade-off management of bias-variance errors. One of the best ways to do the tradeoff analysis is to perform ensemble learning.

The most common methods of ensemble learning are as follows:

- Bagging
- Boosting
- Stacking

In this chapter, we'll focus on Bagging in detail while Boosting will be handled in the next chapter.

What is bagging? How does it work?

Bagging is a method that is used to decrease the variance of the predictions by summing the output of two or more classifiers that are modeled on different samples in the same data set.

The following steps are followed in bagging:

Create Multiple Data sets:

The original data is replaced in sampling with the formation of new data sets.

The new data sets may contain fractions of the rows and columns. These are normally hyper parameters in a bagging model.

If the columns and rows are taken in the fraction that is less than one, it can help to make the model strong and robust. It can also reduce over-fitting.

Build Multiple Classifiers:

These are constructed with each new data set.

Normally the same classifier is constructed on every data set, and the predictions are made later.

Combine Classifiers:

All the predictions of every classifier are combined with the help of a mode, a mean or a median. This depends on the problem on the hand.

The combined values are normally stronger than a single value.

It is important to notice that the number of models that are to be constructed here is not supposed to be a hyper parameter. A greater number of models are almost always better than lower numbers. However, in certain cases, they can also perform on similar planes and thus can give a similar performance to the lower numbers. It is possible to show this theoretically that the variance of all the combined predictions are reduced to $1/n$ where n is the number of classifiers, of the normal variance under certain assumptions.

A variety of implementations of bagging models exist. Random forest is one of such models. It will be discussed it in the next and the last chapter of the decision tree series.

Chapter 6: Decision Trees: Part Three (Random Forests)

In this chapter let us focus on the basics of Random Forests and how it performs its tasks. Random Forest can be called as a universal solution as it is said if you do not know which algorithm to use, you should use a random forest.

The random forest can be defined as a versatile and smart machine learning method that can perform both classifications as well as regression tasks. It can also perform dimensional reduction methods, outlier values, treat missing values and other steps of data exploration as well. It is an expert solution for most of the problems. It is known as an ensemble way of learning as a group of weak models are combined to form this, powerful model.

Workings of Random Forest:

Multiple decision trees are grown in a random forest. This is opposite to the CART model. For the classification of new object based attributes, every one of the trees presents a classification. This presentation is also known as 'voting' for the class. The forest then is given a choice to choose the classification with the most votes.

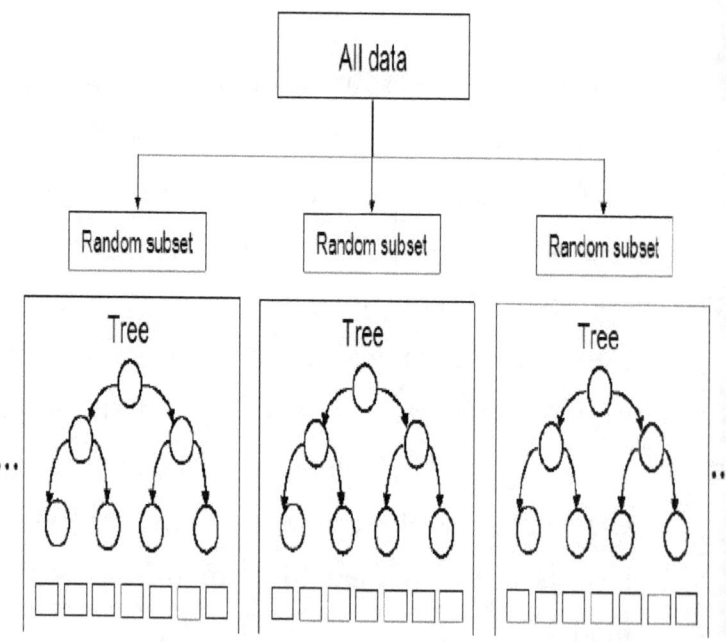

For instance:

Let's say that the number of cases in one training set is N. Then the sample of the N cases can be taken at random. However, it must be replaced. The sample will serve as the training set for the growing tree.

If there exist M input variables then, m<M is specified in a way that at each node, the m variables will be selected at random out of the M. The split will happen on M and m is used to split node.

All the trees are grown as much as they can grow, and no pruning is done.

The prediction of new data takes place by aggregating the other predictions of the ntree.

Advantages of Random Forest

- Random forest algorithm can be used in both sorts of problems. It can be used in regression as well as classification.
- It can handle a large amount of data set in high dimensionality. It can handle more than a few thousands of variables and can very well identify the significant ones among them. It is therefore considered to be an important dimensionality reduction method.
- It can effectively estimate the missing data and can easily maintain accuracy even if it is fed a large amount of data.
- It has various methods that can be used to balance errors in the data set.
- The above features can be used with unlabeled data as well. Thus, it can work unsupervised.
- It samples input data with replacement. This process is known as bootstrap sampling.

Disadvantages of Random Forest

- Like advantages, Random Forest has certain disadvantages too. However, as compared to the disadvantages, the number of advantages is large, thus making Random forests a far better option than other options.
- It is not as good at regression as it is with classification. It often does not come out with precise, continuous nature predictions. It cannot make predictions beyond the range of the provided training data in the case of regression.
- The data may become over-fit if the sample data is too noisy.
- It can act as a black box approach for statistical modelers as you cannot control the performance of the model. You can only try random seeds and different parameters.

What is Boosting? How does it work?

To define in simple terms, boosting is a family of algorithms that transform weak learners to strong or stronger learners.

The definition can be further understood by the use of the following example that deals with spam email identification:

If you are asked to identify Spam and regular mail, what will be the criteria that you will follow to perform your task? Normally, the following steps will be followed:

- If the email contains only one, promotional image: SPAM
- It only has link or links: SPAM
- The body of the email contains only sentences such as "You won a prize money of ---": SPAM
- Email received from an official domain: Not a SPAM
- Email received from a known sender: Not a SPAM

Thus, these are the rules or the criteria that we use to classify whether an email is a spam or not spam. However, do you firmly believe that these criteria are sufficient enough to classify emails in spam and not spam? The answer to the above question is no.

These rules cannot be said to be powerful enough to classify email as spam or not spam on their own. Hence, these rules are known as a weak learner. However, these weak learners can be converted into strong ones by combining the predictions made by the weak learners with the help of various methods such as:

By utilizing average or weighted average

Choosing the prediction that has a higher vote rate.

For instance: In the above example we have five weak learners. If three out of these five are said to be SPAM, then the remaining two will be voted as Not Spam. Therefore, we will continue to consider an email SPAM because the votes are higher in the case.

How does it work?

As we have seen that boosting actually sums the weak learners to form a strong rule. However, the question that should arise in your mind is, how does it identify the weak rules?

To find the weak rule it is necessary to apply the machine-learning algorithm with a varied distribution first. Every time this algorithm is applied, a new weak prediction rule is formed. This is a repetitive process and is repeated many times. The boosting algorithm combines these rules into one single strong prediction rule.

How do we choose a different distribution for each round?

To choose the correct distribution, the following steps can be followed:

1. All the distributions are taken and assigned by the base learner to equal weight and attention.
2. If any prediction error happens due to the first base learning algorithm, more attention is then paid to the observation that has caused the error. It is then applied to the next base-learning algorithm.
3. The second step is repeated until the base learning algorithm limit is reached or a high level of accuracy is gained.

In the last step, it sums up all the results received from the weak learners and makes a strong learner. This learner can improve the prediction power of the model eventually. Boosting is highly focused on mis-classified and high error examples that are preceded by weak rules.

Many boosting algorithms exist that can enhance the accuracy of boosting models even more. Following is a tutorial where you can learn even more about the two most commonly used boosting methods: Gradient Boosting (GBM) and XGBoost.

GBM or XGBoost: Which is more powerful?

Many researchers have admired the boosting capabilities of XGBoost. It often gives out a better output as compared to GBM however, in many cases it is seen that the benefits are less, often inconsequential. XGBoost is better than GBM for the following reasons:

Regularization:

XGBoost has regularization, unlike Standard GBM implementation that has no regularization. Regularization can control the amount of over-fitting. This is why the other name for XGBoost is 'regularized boosting technique.'

Parallel Processing:

Unlike GBM XGBoost has parallel processing, which makes it considerably faster than regular boosting.

A question that might arise in your mind is that how boosting, a serialized or sequential process can be parallelized? This can be explained by the following simple clarification. A decision tree can only be constructed on the base of an older one or a previous one. Hence, it is possible to create or grow a new tree from each core. Thus, it is a versatile method.

XGBoost can also work with Hadoop.

High Flexibility

XGBoost is far more flexible than GBM as it allows the user to optimize and personalize whatever evaluation criteria ass well as optimization objectives that the user wants to change. This makes it highly powerful as it practically removes the limitations from the field and it possible to do whatever you want.

XGBoost is a better option than GBM because it can handle missing values better than GMB. The user can supply a different value that is not the observation and can pass it as a parameter. XGBoost will try to perform different tasks as it can locate a missing value on every node and can learn the path as well.

Tree Pruning:

A GBM often stops splitting nodes when it locates a negative loss in the split. Therefore, it is considered to be a greedier algorithm. Compared to GBM, XGBoost can split till the max_depth of the value is achieved and then it starts the pruning mechanism where it removes the splits, going backward when it cannot find a positive gain.

Built-in Cross-Validation

XGBoost has a built in mechanism of cross-validation that is run at the each repetition. Thus, it becomes extremely easy to derive the perfect number of boosting repetitions in a single run. This is not seen in the case of GBM where you have to run a grid-search, and only some specific values get tested in the mechanism.

Continuing the Existing Model

It possible to start the XGBoost model from any last iteration in the last run. This is highly important in certain applications.

How to work with GBM in R and Python?

It is necessary to understand the necessary parameters before we have a look at the algorithm itself. These can be used in R as well as Python.

Following is the pseudo-code of GBM algorithm for two classes:

Start the outcome.

1. Repeat from 1 to the actual number of trees.

2. Add the weights for the targets after each run. These will be based on the previous run itself.

2.1. Fix the model on the selected data subsample.

2.2. Perform predictions till a full set of observation is done.

2.3. Update the results with the current results. Identify the learning rate.

3. Return the last output.

Although this is a basic and very naïve explanation of GBM, yet it will help the beginners to understand the workings of the algorithm.

Now let us have a look at the parameters that are used in Python:

learning_rate

This identifies the impact of every single tree on the final result. GBM begins the work by initializing the starting estimate. This is then updated with the help of result of all the subsequent trees. The learning parameter is used to control the magnitude of the change that is seen in the estimates.

In this example, lower values are more appreciated as they can make the model stronger to certain characteristics of the tree. This allows them to generalize well.

n_estimators

This stands for the number of sequential trees that need to be modeled. GBM is quite robust at a large number of trees. However, it may over-fit at a certain point. Hence, this parameter is used to tune the learning rate.

Subsample

This is the fraction of observations that are to be chosen for every tree. This is performed using random sampling.

Values that are less than 1 can make the model strong by slowing down the variance. Generally, values of ~0.8 used and work great.

Apart from the above mentioned, there are certainly other parameters that can be used to enhance the performance of the method.

Loss

It is in reference to the loss function. This is to be minimized with each split.

This parameter can have many values for both, regression and classification. Normally the default values are used. Other values are to be used only if you understand their role.

Init

This parameter affects the initialization of the output. It can be used if another model whose result is to be used as the initial estimates for GBM has been constructed.

random state

This is the random number seed due to which the same random numbers get generated whenever they are used.

This parameter is necessary for tuning. If a random number is not fixed, then we cannot have different results for all the following runs on the same parameters. This makes it difficult to compare the models.

Verbose

This refers to the type of output that is to be printed when the model fits well. The values can be varied, and they are as follows:

1. 0: No sort of result is generated. This is the default value.
2. 1: Result is generated at only certain intervals for the trees.
3. >1: Result is generated for all the trees.

warm_start

This is an interesting parameter, and it can help the user in a significant way if it is used judicially and properly. This parameter can be used to fit extra trees on the previous models with ease. This will allow you to save a lot of time and thus allow you to conduct various advanced applications.

Presort

This is used when you need to choose whether to presort the data for quicker splits. It creates an automatic selection by default. However, the values can be changed if necessary.

For R users who use caret package these are the main tuning parameters:

- N.trees – This is the number of repetitions and the tree that will be used to grow the subsequent trees.
- Interaction.depth – It identifies the complexity of the tree or the total number of splits that the tree has to perform.
- Shrinkage – This is used in the reference of learning rate. It similar to the learning rate as presented in python.

- N.minobsinnode – It is the minimum number of training samples that are needed for a node to continue splitting.

Where to practice?

To master any skill or concept, it is necessary to practice regularly. Similarly, you also need to practice regularly if you want to master the above-mentioned algorithms.

Practicing is easy for the above-mentioned algorithms as there are many online services where you can find practice games and tests. These tests are updated frequently, and you can also participate in a variety of competitions that can help you master algorithms. These competitions often feature a global level leaderboard, so not only can you practice your algorithms, but also can show off your skills and progress to the whole world. You can also find offline practice sets that can be used to practice when you cannot connect to the Internet.

Thus, here ends the three part series of Decision Tree learning series in this book. In the next chapter, let us have a look at some other forms of machine learning that becoming highly popular in today's world.

Chapter 7: Deep Learning

Till now we have discussed the basics of machine learning and the basics and working so f decision trees and random forests as well. However, it is clear that the field of machine learning does not end here; rather it grows in size as well as complications hereafter. One of the major concepts that are becoming highly popular nowadays is Deep learning. This chapter will serve as a minor introduction to this method of learning.

Deep learning or hierarchical learning is said to be the use of non-biological neural networks to study and learn the aspects that have one or more than one hidden layers. It is situated in the learning data representations. In the method, the learning can be totally supervised, partially supervised or not supervised at all.

The architectures of deep belief system, deep learning system, recurrent neural networks as well as deep neural networks all are used and applied in many fields including computer vision, speech recognition, machine translation, social network filtering, natural language processing, bioinformatics, sound recognition, etc. Here these methods give out outputs that can easily compete with the results that are given out by human users.

Deep learning thus is a family or class of machine learning algorithm that uses a cascade of more than two layers of nonlinear processing units for feature extraction and transformation. These layers are cascading and nested therefore the output, or the result of the last layer becomes the input or the sample for the next or following layer. These can be supervised or unsupervised, ex- classification and pattern analysis. The unsupervised ones use multifaceted levels of data. They also use the representations of the data. The method is nested here where the higher level features are based on, the lower level features.

The World School Council of London first designed deep learning.

The difference between Machine Learning, Deep Learning, and AI:

The main difference or rather the main characteristic difference between the above-mentioned three concepts is that Deep learning is a type of machine learning whereas machine learning is a form of AI or artificial intelligence. Machine learning is considered to be the most popular approaches or forms of artificial intelligence. However, not all of the systems based on AI use machine learning, for instance, self-driven or automatic cars use rule-based systems.

It has been prophesized that in the coming future machine learning will be the most prominent form of AI.

Deep learning can be defined as a type or kind of approach towards machine learning that is extremely popular and advanced.

Though the future of machine learning is bright, however, it is not concrete. If another technique is invented that turns out to be better than machine learning, it will be replaced as soon as possible, without any issue.

Chapter 8: Digital Neural Network and Computer Science

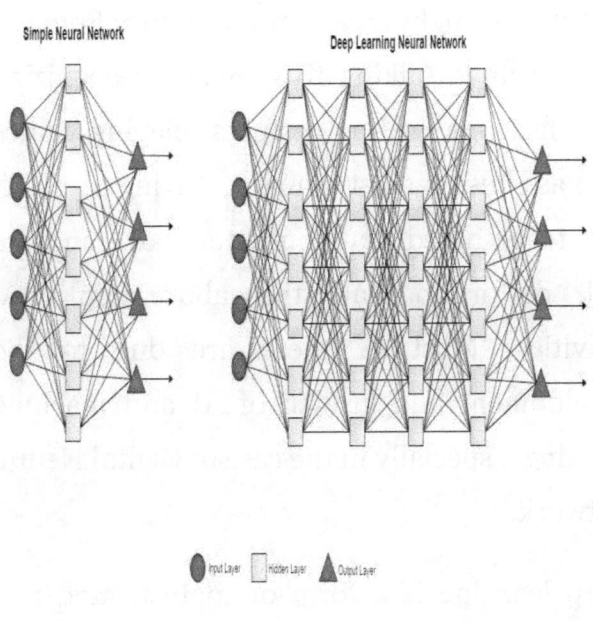

(Enlarged Legend)

The modern computer and computing were invented in the 20th century. People everywhere have guessed and tried to speculate the achievements and innovations that the computers might create in the future. Some of them include talking to humans, recognizing their faces as well as gestures, playing games such as chess against humans, driving cars, etc. It is to be noted that computers have and are still performing all the above-mentioned activities. Most of these are due to the development and growth of AI and machine learning, especially in the case of Digital Neural Network.

Deep learning is a form of sophisticated and highly developed form of neural networks. These were first developed and used about 70 years ago. Two scientists, Walter Pitts and Warren McCullough in 1944, first thought of the idea. However, the research soon changed its trajectory, and it stopped developing.

However, in the 90s it rose again, and now it is considered to be the most important concept in the AI.

Artificial neural networks are also known as ANN are computing systems that are based on biological neural networks commonly seen in the brains of animals, especially animals. Thus, it is an imitation of the intricate system of neurons that have been developed by nature.

The best feature of this system is that it learns and performs tasks by inspecting examples without the need of task-specific programming. This thus decreases the time as well as the resources that are required.

An ANN group is constructed of multiple artificial neurons. These are connected with each other where the connections are used to transmit and transfer signals from one neuron to the other. They are also organized in multiple layers. Each of these layers performs a different and varied function. The signals normally travel many times through the whole set.

The biggest goal of ANN is the imitation of the human brain and the methods that are used by the human brain to solve these problems. However, nowadays the focus of ANN is changing and now it is more concentrated on the problem solving itself and not on imitating the neural networks. This is why scientists are coming up with many techniques and networks that are quite different than the natural ones but are far more powerful than the regular ones.

Applications of ANN

ANN is used in applications such as

- Solar energy to model and design better gadgets and appliances.
- Also used in system modeling.

- Can easily handle complicated and incomplete data.
- Can be used to solve nonlinear problems.
- Air conditioning systems
- Ventilation
- Refrigeration
- Heating
- Power Generation
- Load forecasting
- Estimation of heating loads in buildings and construction.
- Robotics
- Forecasting
- Pattern Recognition
- Medicine
- Manufacturing
- Social and psychological sciences
- Signal processing
- Optimization.
- Prediction of air flow

- Prediction of consumption of energy in a solar building.

Thus, it can be seen that artificial neural network can work wonders in the field of computers.

Advantages of ANN

- The neural network is able to perform tasks that cannot be performed by the linear network.
- As it is a nonlinear network, even if one or more elements fail, the network still continues to process and work.
- It need not be reprogrammed again and again.
- It is easy to use.
- It is an adaptive method of learning. It is highly robust and can solve a variety of difficult problems with relative ease. Can be used in a variety of applications.
- The advantages of ANN are far more than the disadvantages of risks that are associated with the technology.

- It uses simple samples to come up with results and responses.
- It is extremely flexible and adaptable. It can learn easily with very fewer variables.
- It is more forgiving to the user generated errors and thus is much more suitable than a linear network.
- Based on adaptive learning.

Risks associated with ANN

There are certain risks involved while using ANN. However, it can be seen that the list of advantages is much longer the list of risks:

- A user needs a lot of training to learn how to use ANN properly. However, once learned, it is quite easy to use.
- It is a time-consuming process.
- The architecture is different than microprocessor hence proper emulation is needed before using ANN.

Types of Artificial Neural Networks

Multiple types of ANN or artificial neural exists, out these, the following three are important.

- Feedback ANN: The result goes into the network itself, and the process gets repeated until the perfect result or output is achieved.
- Feed Forward ANN: It is a simple network. It contains an output layer, an input layer and one or more layer of neurons
- Classification Prediction ANN: It is a subset of the feed forward artificial neural network.

Summary:

The goal of AI (Artificial intelligence) is to mimic human capabilities, such as knowledge application, abstract thinking, reasoning, etc. On the contrary machine learning operates on the principles of using writing software based on past experiences.

To our surprise machine learning in actual fact is very similarly related to data mining and statistics as oppose to AI. Why is that? In essence when a computer program performs a particular task based on experiences from the past, than we can conclude the machine has "learnt". This is much different from a program performing a task as its' programmers have comprehensively defined its capacities already.

Machine learning can be placed into 3 distinct categories:

Supervised Learning - Teach and train machines with data that is already labeled with the correct answers and outcomes. The more data available the more the machine will learn from the given topic or subject matters. For instance, an apple is red, banana yellow , and broccoli is green. After the machine is trained it is given new unseen data and the learning algorithm uses its past experiences to determine an outcome.

Unsupervised Learning- when a machine is trained with data sets that do not have labels. The learning algorithm is not told what the data represents. So for example, here is a letter or an apple, but no further information is given on its details. Or perhaps describing characteristic of a certain object, like a tree, but not giving the label of its name.

So how does this work? Imagine listening to a podcast of a foreign language like Mandarin or Hindi. You listen to hundreds upon hundreds of podcasts and start to establish patterns, form models, and recognize certain sounds. - Unsupervised learning operates much in the same way.

Reinforcement Learning- similar to unsupervised learning, the data is not labeled. But when asked a question of the data, the outcome will be evaluated. So for instance, imagine playing against a computer in the game of chess.

When the computer wins it than evaluates the result to validate how it won and thus reinforces the action. Ergo, when the computer engages in playing thousands of games it collectively establishes a strategy and framework in winning.

There is this buzz word "Neural Net" we hear of in the world of machine learning, but what is it exactly? Its modeled after our brain neural networks and operates synonymously to a neuron. When a given number of inputs are given the neural will propagate a signal depending on how it interprets it.

The Above mentioned in this summary sub chapter is the fundamental concepts of machine learning. This is how machine learning functions and operates, and much of what we utilize today without even knowing it!

Conclusion

This is the era of technology, and thus it is changing and evolving every day. Every day, it is becoming extremely difficult to keep up with the new innovations, latest trends, discoveries and inventions in almost every field. This is especially true in the case of science and technology. Science and technology are the two fields that are developing the most rapidly in today's world. Hence, to keep up with such a never seen before pace, a person needs to be extremely up to date and techno-savvy. However, this not possible for everyone. Hence, books like this one help general population to understand the basics of the current buzzwords and concepts, so that they can be relevant. This book is an attempt to serve such population by helping them understand the basics of machine learning, AI, and decision trees in simple and lucid manner.

The book is best suited for beginners in who are interested in machine learning. However, you can also find information that is suitable for adepts as well. For the ease of the general reader, the language of the book has been kept simple and relatively jargon free. The book is divided into multiple sections so that you can only read the sections that are important for you.

The main concern of this book, tree based algorithms is highly important for all sort of scientists that deal with data. They are known to provide the best performing model as compared to other models in the machine learning family. In this book, different aspects of decision trees and random forests have been discussed. Tree based modeling has been discussed from scratch. I am sure that you must have learned the importance of decision tree and how a biological concept is being used to upgrade the technology.

I am sure that this book will act as a basic guide for everyone who is interested in AI. As stated earlier, it is written in a simple and lucid manner, so it suitable for every member of your family. As an added bonus, a few chapters have been dedicated to deep learning and neural networking. These will help as a guide if you want to study advanced machine learning. I also hope that this book has done away with any myths that you had about machine learning and AI.

Once again thank you for buying this book and good luck!

If you enjoyed reading this book please leave a quality review on Amazon. It would be very helpful and appreciated. Link below...

LINK: http://amzn.to/2xCDN19

Other recommended books:

Markov Models

LINK: http://amzn.to/2ey04bI

Data Analytics Beginners Guide

LINK: http://amzn.to/2iNsCiQ

Thank you.

BONUS - DATA ANALYTICS INTRODUCITON

Table of Contents

Introduction

Chapter 1: Regression Analysis

Chapter 2: Big Data

Chapter 3: Data and Text Mining

Chapter 4: Data Management

Chapter 5: Data Reduction and Clustering

Chapter 6: Web Scraping

Chapter 7: Data Analysis in the Real World

Chapter 8: Social Network Analysis

Chapter 9: Data Analysis Techniques

Conclusion

financial, medical or professional advice. Please consult a licensed professional before attempting any techniques outlined in this book.

By reading this document, the reader agrees that under no circumstances are is the author responsible for any losses, direct or indirect, which are incurred as a result of the use of information contained within this document, including, but not limited to, —errors, omissions, or inaccuracies

Introduction

Congratulations on purchasing/downloading this book !

The following chapters we'll discuss are going to inform you of everything that you need to know in order to analyze data. Whenever you are analyzing data, you are going to be taking data and modifying it, inspecting it, creating models of the data, and even cleaning up the data so that it can be used in the equations that you need to use it in.

Data analytics is used in the real world in a lot of jobs that you may be looking to get yourself into. In order to get yourself into data analytics and get hired into a job that will pay you more money, you are going to want to ensure that you have everything that you need to know under your belt so that you are placing yourself one step ahead of the competition and get yourself hired!

When you are doing data analysis, you are going to be taking raw data that you gathered from your sources and turning it into information that you are going to find more useful not only to you, but to others too. All of the data that you collect is going to come from you answering a question or testing a hypothesis or even when you are trying to disprove a theory.

You are going to have to keep in mind that there are going to be multiple phases that you are going to go through in order to work with the data that you collect so that it can be analyzed correctly. You should not be surprised if one of the phases means that there is going to be extra work on your end in previous steps so that you are getting the appropriate data analysis.

At the point in time that data is placed into an analysis program, you are going to have to go on the parameters that are set into place either by you or the person who is making the decisions to make sure that you are making sure that your consumer is getting an excellent product.

Most of the data that you are going to be analyzing is going to be collected through an innovative process such as going to a particular area in a neighborhood and collecting information from that specific community. From there, the variables are going to be broken down based on the individuals who fit into groups such as age, income, so on and so forth. Your data is going to categorical or numerical depending on what you are trying to figure out.

As you go about collecting your data, you are going to need to follow all of the requirements that are going to keep you on track for the study. In other words, you are not going to want to ask about someone's favorite movie when you are trying to discover how many children they have. There are going to be sensors that you are going to use such as traffic cameras or environmental sensors that are going to give you all of the data that you want to know. Not only that, but you can do an interview face to face in order to obtain the data that you need.

Once you have collected all of the data that you need, then you are going to be at the step where you are going to be ready to share the data that you have analyzed. In the end, the result is going to require that you get feedback from your consumer so that you can help make sure that your company is running more efficiently so that you can ensure that you are getting the product out to the customer that they are wanting. In other words, you are going to be making sure that you are not putting out a defective product that no one is going to buy.

There are going to be times that you are going to have to use visualization tools to make sure that you are sharing the data in a way that everyone understands. Not everyone is going to be able to understand the data by being told a variety of number.

There are plenty of books on this subject on the market, thanks again for choosing this one! Every effort was made to ensure it is full of as much useful information as possible, please enjoy!

Description

Data analytics is used in the real world in a lot of jobs that you may be looking to get yourself into. In order to get yourself into data analytics and get hired into a job that will pay you more money, you are going to want to ensure that you have everything that you need to know under your belt so that you are placing yourself one step ahead of the competition and get yourself hired!

The chapter discussions of this book are going to inform you of everything that you need to know in order to analyze data.

These include :

- Things you need to know about regression analysis and social network analysis

- What are big data, data and text mining, and web scraping and their applications in the real world
- Techniques in data analysis
- Learn how to reduce your workload through data reduction
- Risks that you have to know in order to protect yourself, your company, and your data
- And so much more...

Chapter 1: Regression Analysis

When dealing with statistical models, you are going to use regression analysis. Regression analysis is a process that you are going to be determining what relationships there are amongst all of the variables that are being used. Using techniques such as modeling and analyzing the variables will be included whenever the focus is on the relationship that falls between the independent and the dependent variables.

In other words, regression analysis is going to assist the user in understanding that how the usual value for the dependent variable is going to change whenever one of the independent variables remains unchanged while other independent variables are changed. Estimating the conditional expectation for the dependent variable depending on what the independent variable is one of the most common regression analysis.

The less common use is going to be on quantile or the location parameter for the distribution of the dependent variable given what independent variables are being used. Nonetheless, all cases when regression analysis is used is going to be to target the function of the independent variables.

Regression models

There are three variables that all regression models will have.

Your dependent variable will be y.

The independent variable will be x.

Finally, the unknown parameters are going to be denoted with the beta symbol. Which is going to be represented as the scalar or the vector.

There are going to be a lot of different fields for applications which are going to consist of various terms that are going to be used to describe the independent and dependent variables.

Regression models are going to relate the dependent variable to the function of the independent variable and the unknown parameters.

$Y \approx f(x, \beta) Y \approx f(x, \beta)$

In other words, it is going to be formalized as

$E(Y|X) = f(x, \beta)$

This is done in order to carry out the regression analysis. In each expression, f has to be specified. There are going to be times that this form is going to be based on the information that you gathered about the connection between x and y while it does not depend on the data that you have obtained. If there is no knowledge available, there is going to be a convenient or flexible form that f is going to be chosen for.

You are going to assume now that the vector for your parameters of beta is going to be the length of k. So, the user is going to have to provide the information for the dependent variable to be able to get a regression analysis.

In the event that the n data points for y and x are observed, then n is going to be less than k in most of the classical approaches that you are going to see in regression analysis and if this happens, then there will be no performed analysis. This happens because the equations' system is going to define the regressions model for the undetermined. There is also not going to be enough data for you to be able to recover beta.

If n is equal to the k data points, then the function of f will end up being linear. Your equation is going to be $y = f(X, \beta) y = f(X, \beta)$ which is going to be able to able to be solved exactly rather than give you an approximation. Therefore, you are going to be reducing your work because you are only going to be solving the n set of equations in which n's unknowns are going to be the elements of beta. As long as x is linearly independent, there will always be a unique solution. Therefore, the solution is not going to exist or there are going to be multiple solutions in case f will be nonlinear.

Another common situation you are going to see is when n is greater than the k data points that are being observed. If you find yourself working with this situation then there is going to be enough information in your hands to be able to estimate what the value of beta is going to best fit the data that you are working with. So, your regression model is going to be viewed as an over determined system inside of beta.

When working with the last regression analysis that was mentioned you are going to have the tools provided to you so that you can find a solution for your parameters of beta. Not only that, but under some statistical assumptions, the analysis is going to use the extra data that you have so that you can predict what your dependent variable is.

Independent measurements

When looking at regression models, there are going to be three unknown parameters. If you look at an experiment where there are ten measurements that are all the same value for the independent variable vector X, there is going to be that many independent variables. So, for this example, there are going to be three independent variables.

In this instance, the regression analysis is going to fail to result in a unique set of values that were estimated for the parameters this experiment did not provide you with enough data. Therefore, you can estimate the average value and the standard deviation for your dependent variables.

On the same hand, you are going to be measuring two different values for your independent variable in order to get enough information for the regression of two of your parameters but not for three or more of those that you do not know.

If there had been different measurements with three different values, then you would have received a unique set of estimations for your parameters.

Therefore, you are going to strive to have different numbered measurements so that you can figure out what your beta is going to be.

Underlying assumptions

Some of the more classical assumptions that you are going to see in data analysis are:

1. The samples that are going to be representative of the population of the inference predictions.
2. If there is an error it is going to be the random variable which is going to mean

that you have zero conditions on the analytical variables.

3. Without errors, your independent variables are going to be measured. Keep in mind that if this does not happen, then the modeling can be done rather than using an error in variables model.

4. Independent variables will be linearly independent which means it is not possible to show the predictors as a linear combination.

5. Errors are going to be uncorrelated which means that your variance covariance matrix for your errors is going to be diagonal and every element that is not zero will be a variance of the error that you are seeing.

6. Variance for the errors will be constant across all of your observations. If you find that this is not the case, then you can use the weighted least squares method.

Power and simple sized calculations

When talking about regression analysis, there are not any methods that have been agreed upon when it comes to the number of independent variables against the number of observations that you are going to find inside of a model. One rule that you are going to want to try and follow is $N = m^n$ in which n is going to be the size of the sample, the superscript n is going to be how many independent variables there are in the equation, and m is how many observations that are needed in order to reach the precision that you want.

Take for example that there is a researcher that is trying to build a linear regression model by using the data that they collected from over a thousand different patients in their local hospital. The number of patients is going to be N. but, what happens if the researcher decides to take five of those thousand observations and decides that they need to create a straight line? This is going to be the m in your equation because the maximum number of independent variables that you are going to be able to have is 4.

Log 1000/log 5 = 4.29

Other methods to use with regression analysis

Because the parameters that you find in a regression model are typically going to be an estimation due to the method used. Some of these methods are:

1. The Bayesian method or the Bayesian linear regression
2. Distance metric learning. You are going to learn this by searching for the meaningful distance metric inside of any given input space.

3. Percentage regression. You are going to find that for most situations where you are reducing the percentage errors to find the one that is more appropriate.
4. Nonparametric regression. This method is going to require a lot of observations and is going to be intensive when it comes to the calculations.
5. Least absolute deviations are going to be one of the more robust outlines which are going to end up leading you into doing quantile regression.

Other Recommended Books

Machine Learning

LINK: http://amzn.to/2xCDN19

Markov Models

LINK: http://amzn.to/2ey04b

Chapter 2: Big Data

You are going to come to realize that big data is going to be the term that you are going to use for the data sets that are larger and more complex than the standard data processing application software is able to deal with. The challenges that come with big data are going to be the capturing of data, the visualization querying, sharing, transferring, data storage, data analysis, and the information privacy for the data that you are working with.

Big data applications

Big data has grown in its demand for information that different management specialists have needed in order to keep their business up and going. Some of these businesses are Microsoft, Dell, Software AG, Oracle Corporation and more. These companies have spent over fifteen billion dollars on software firms for the specialization of data management and analytics.

The big data business back in 2010 was worth over a hundred billion dollars and has continued to grow about 10%annually, which is two times faster than the software industry as a whole.

The government uses and adopts big data inside of their processes to allow for efficiencies in terms of innovation, productivity, and costs. However, this does not mean that there are not any flaws in the process of using big data. The use of data analysis is going to require several various parts of the government at once to work together and create the new processes that are needed in order to get the outcome that they are wanting.

United States of America

1. In 2012, the Obama administration said that in order to see how big data could help to address some of the bigger issues that the government was dealing with, data research and development was going to be used.
2. It was big data that helped to get Barack Obama reelected to his presidency.
3. The federal government has six of the ten supercomputers that can be found in the world.
4. The National Security Agency built Utah data center and whenever they were done, they were able to handle massive amounts of data that was collected by the NSA over the world wide web. No one knows how much space there is for storing big data.

India

1. Big data helped to win the Indian general election that took place in 2014.
2. The government in India uses various techniques in order to ascertain exactly how the Indian electorate will respond to the government's actions.

United Kingdom

1. Big data for prescription drugs ties together the location, time, and origin of each prescription in their country. This helps to see what drugs are being used on the general patient.
2. Joining the data with the local authority about things like road gritting and meals on wheels services allows for the local authority to miss the weather-related delays that they have to watch out for.

International development

There has been research how effective big data can be used for ICT4D or the Information and Communication Technologies for Development. ICT4D proposes that big data does not only make a great improvement but also brings up some exceptional challenges when it comes to worldwide advancement.

There have been advancements in the analysis of big data which offers a more cost-effective opportunity so that it can improve the decision making that has to happen in the most critical development areas like health care, crime, and natural disaster.

On top of that, there has been data generated from users to offer new opportunities to those that are often unheard. But, there are some longstanding challenges that have appeared from the developing regions where there are inadequate technological infrastructures and human resources are limited.

Finance

Big data in finance is known as technical analysis. There are some nonfinancial data on the financial market which assists in making predictions known as alternative data. This means that the data that is non-financial is going to be what helps to make financial decisions because finances are going to affect more than just the economy and how it works.

Manufacturing

According to the TCS 2013 Global Trend Study, there have been some big improvements in supply planning and the quality of a product in order to provide the biggest benefit of big data that can be used for manufacturing.

A foundation for the transparency that is needed in the manufacturing industry has been provided by big data, which enables them to unravel the uncertainties like inconsistent component performance and the availability of a product.

So that it can be turned into useful data, the predictive manufacturing process has a near zero downtime and the transparency needs the advancement of prediction tools and a lot of data for a more systematic processing. This is an abstract structure for the predictive manufacturing that starts with the acquisition of data where there are diverse types of sensory data that are ready to obtain various voltage, pressure, acoustics, and more.

All of the historical data along with the sensory data will create the big data that is required in manufacturing. Whenever big data is generated, it is going to act as an input for the predictive tools and preventive strategies that you are going to use like Prognostics health management.

Cyber physical models

Currently, Prognostics health management uses data while they are working with it while allowing the analytical algorithms to perform the calculations so that they get more accurate results whenever there is enough information to input into the machine during its lifecycle. Some things that are going to be put in is the physical knowledge that someone knows or the system configurations.

Sometimes there has to be a systematic integrate so that data can be managed and analyzed before it is processed during the various stages that the machine is going to go through in its life cycle so that it can deal with data more effectively.

Whenever there is motivation, there is going to be a cyber physical model being developed because the model is going to be coupled with the motivation. Because of this coupled model, there is going to be a digital twin of the real machine that is going to operate in the cloud so that it can simulate the health conditions of the machine as well as the data that is inputted into it. This can best be described as a 5s systematic approach that is going to consist of the service, synthesis, synchronization, storage, and sensing of the data.

A digital image from the early design stage will be built by the model that is joined. During the product's design, the physical knowledge and system's information will be logged which is going to end up being based on the simulation model that is built as a reference for the future analysis.

There will be a generalization of the initial parameters which is going to make it to where they are turned into the data so it can be utilized for manufacturing or testing.

Health care

Big data analytics helps health care to improve by providing clinical risk interventions, waste and care reduction, and personalized medicine and prescriptive analysis. There are still some areas where improvements are going to be seen more than others because the improvement is going to be aspirational instead of implemented.

There are levels of data that is generated inside of the health care system and none of it is going to be trivial. The volume of the data that is coming in is going to continue to increase with the new adoptions of e-Health and m-Health (mobile health), and even wearable technology.

This makes it to where there is a greater need for those who can pay attention to this data and analyze it so that people are getting the best health care possible.

Education

There was a study conducted at McKinsey Global Institute that found there is a shortage of those who are trained to deal with big data by about one point five million people, this also includes the number of universities as well. This is why various universities such as UC Berkeley have created master's programs in order to train people to try and meet the demand that there is for big data.

There have even been private boot camps developed in order to help meet the demand.

Media

Big data is used in the media by showing those in media jobs what they should report on in order to reach their views and readers. However, there has been a shift in media where it appears to be moving away from the traditional approach of using newspapers and television shows. Now, they are going to social media and looking at what people are talking about and posting about. This is used so that they can target specific audiences with advertisements and articles that are found in the newspapers and magazines that are picked up by the consumer.

In fact, Channel 4 is a British public service television broadcaster and it is one of the biggest leaders in big data and data analysis.

Chapter 3: Data and Text Mining

Data mining is going to be the process of looking and discovering patterns in large sets of data by using methods that can be located at the intersection of statistics, database systems, and machine learning. This is an interdisciplinary subfield of computer science where the ultimate goal is to extract the information that is needed from a data set and then modify it so that it can be understood and used later.

There are at least six different classes that you are going to see in data mining.

1. Anomaly detection which is the detection of unusual data records. This is going to be where you are going to discover errors in your data which may end up causing you to have to look

further into the error to see how you can change it and make your data produce the outcome that you are wanting.

2. Association rule learning is going to look for the various relationships that can be found between variables. Take for example how a store is going to obtain the various purchasing habits of a customer in order to learn which products they should keep in their store and what they can get rid of so they can bring in new products for their customers.

3. The cluster will be the task that you use in order to discover structures and groups inside of your data that are similar to each other without using any known structures in the data.

4. Classification will be when you generalize the structure that you know about so you can apply new data. Take for example how your email program is

going to filter out your emails between legitimate and spam.
5. Regression, as we discussed earlier, is going to be the function that will model the data with the least errors that can be found all while estimating the relationships that can be found between the data and the data sets.
6. Summarization is going to give you some compact representation of the data set that you are working with. This is going to include the report generation.

Result validation

Even if you do not mean to, data mining can end up being misused which then can make results seem like they are significant, however, they cannot be reproduced onto a new sample of data because they are not going to actually predict the future behavior which means that they bare very little use. Many times, While not doing the accurate statistical hypothesis testing, the results, many times, are going to come from investigating too many hypotheses.

You can see a simple version of this in over fitting, however, the same problem has been known to arise during distinct phases of the process which can cause a split when applicable, test, or train, but it may not be enough to stop this from happening.

One of the final steps in knowledge discovery for over fitting is going to come from the data being able to verify which patterns have been created by the mining algorithms which can appear in the larger data set. You are going to have to use a test set for the data which your data mining algorithm is not going to be trained in order to overcome over fitting like this. The patterns that are learned are going to apply to the test set and going to result in an output that is going to be carried to the output that you were wanting.

Take for example a data mining algorithm that tries to tell the difference between spam emails and legitimate emails. This is going to be learned by the algorithm by using a training set of emails. After the algorithm has been trained to tell the difference, then its accuracy is going to be measured by how many emails are sent to the correct folder.

Standards

The standards needed for the data mining process have been tried to be defined by those who use data mining. For instance, they released CRISP-DMor Cross Industry Standard Process for Data Mining back in '99, as well as in 2004 the Java Data Mining standard was put out there for the public to use in data analysis. These processes were made active in 2006 but have been stalled ever since because a final draft has not been reached.

The key is going to be Predictive Model Markup language in exchange for the extracted models like predictive analytics. The Data Mining Group developed this XML language. This language was supported as an exchange format by multiple data mining applications. It is only going to work with prediction models, just like the name suggests, where a certain data mining task has been set of great significance for applications in the business.

But, there are extensions that can be used to cover the subspace clustering having been proposed independent from the data mining group.

Notable uses

You are going to see data mining everywhere around you. Some of the biggest industries where you are going to see it is science and health care.

With science, it is obvious that data is going to be collected from the testing of hypotheses in order to make things better and more efficient. Such as, rocket fuel that is going to last longer and still get the shuttle to where its destination. Data is going to be collected from the various tests that are done on the various kinds of rocket fuel to see if it can be changed over to something that is more cost effective.

With health care, data is used to provide individualized health care to each person. This is done because not everyone is going to be coming in due to the fact that they have a sore throat. Not only that, but you cannot treat a heart attack or a stroke the same way that you would a gunshot wound. So, data has to be collected from the patient in order to give the best treatment that there is.

Privacy concerns and ethics

Even though the actual term data mining is not going to have any ethical implications it is still often referred to as the mining of information that relates to people's behavior.

The ways that the information from data mining is used has caused privacy concerns as well as ethics and legality issues to be brought up. One of the biggest concerns is how the data from data mining is being used by the commercial data sets or the government for things like law enforcement purposes or for the national security.

Data mining brings up the need for data preparation which has the possibility of uncovering information or patterns that can end up compromising the privacy obligations and confidentiality. Using data aggregation is one way for this to possibly happen. The aggregation of data is going to involve combining the data together in such a way that it is going to facilitate an analysis.

Data aggregation is not necessarily data mining, but as a result of the preparation of data before and the purpose of that data, it can cause a threat to one's privacy once all the data has been compiled because the miner now has access to the new data set and is going to be able to pick out specific pieces of information whereas before the data left the user anonymous.

That is why it is endorsed that people should be informed of what the data is going to going to be used for before the data is even collected.

Text mining

Also known as text data mining, text mining is going to be equivalent to text analytics. It typically involves structuring the input and finding the patterns inside of that structured data before interpreting the output. Text mining is the method of getting high-quality information from a proved text. High-quality in text mining is going to refer to the combination of the novelty, most relevant, and most appealing in the text. The high-quality information is going to be pulled from the constructing of trends and patterns through things like statistical pattern learning.

Text analysis involves the lexical analysis used to study the recognizing patterns, the word frequency distributions, so on and so forth and the retrieval of information. The overarching goal is going to be to take that text and turn it into data for analysis through the application of natural language processing and analytical methods.

Text analysis processes

There are subtasks that you are going to use in the larger text analytics such as:

1. Identification of corpus or the retrieval of information. This is a preparatory step which you are going to use to identify of gather the set of textual materials that are found inside of a file system or on the internet.
2. Because some text analytics systems are going to implement exclusively to more advanced statistical methods where others are going to implement more expanded analysis.
3. The named entity recognition will be used for the gazetteers or the statistical technique in order to identify the named text features such as names, symbols so on and so forth. disambiguation is going to use contextual clues that may end up being required in order to decide what the text is referring to.
4. Recognition of pattern identified entities are going to be features like email addresses or phone numbers which can

be determined through similarity of patterns or common expressions.

5. The Noun phrases and other terms that can all point to the same object will be identified by the co-reference.

6. The relationships and facts extraction are going to identify the associations through the entities found in the text.

7. Sentiment analysis is going to include the discerning subjective material as well as the extracting of various forms of attitudinal information. The text analytics techniques for this are going to assist in analyzing the sentiment pointed at the entity.

8. Quantitative text analysis will be the set of techniques that are used but they are going to be stemmed from the social sciences wherein a computer or a human is going to extract the semantic or grammatical connections between words to discover the meaning of the stylistic arrangement for a casual personal text

for things such as psychological profiling.

Applications

With technology as advanced as it is, it works not just for private use, but for the government, research and even the needs of businesses. The applications can be sorted into categories and then analyzed by type or function. If you use this approach, then you can classify solutions. Some of the application categories may be things like:

1. Social media monitoring
2. Enterprise business intelligence and data mining
3. Search and informative access
4. E-discovery and records management
5. Automated ad placement
6. Publishing
7. National security and intelligence

8. Publishing

And so much more.

Security applications

A lot of the text mining software packages are marketed to those who use security applications for things like monitoring or analysis of the internet for national security purpose. This is also going to work for the encryption and decryption of files.

Biomedical applications

There are a lot of different applications that are going to be used for text mining when it comes to biomedical literature. One application that you can find online is going to be known as PubGene. This application is going to combine the biomedical text mining with the visualization of the network on an internet service.

If you are searching for biomedical texts, a search engine known as GoPubMed can be used.

Software applications

The software and method that you use for text mining are going to be developed and researched by some of the bigger firms such as Microsoft so that they can further automate the processes and work in different areas of searching and indexing so that the results are improved.

An effort has been placed on creating software in the public sector so that terroristic activities can be monitored and tracked which is important to stop and intercept terrorist attacks.

Online media applications

Many large media companies like the Tribune company is using text mining for them to be able to gather information from their readers and this information will then be used to improve search experiences. This, in turn, increases the site's revenue and a lot of readers stick around because of the relevance of the search results.

An added plus is that the editors are able to package and share news through features that are going to increase the opportunities to monetize content that is placed on their site.

In making their site more effective, they are going to obtain more readers because they know what their readers want to see.

Business and marketing applications

Text mining is used for customer relationship management and marketing. Text mining is used to improve the predictive analytics models for customer attribution. It can also be applied to the stock returns predictions.

Sentiment analysis

This type of analysis is going to include analysis of things such as movie reviews so that it can be estimated on how favorable a review is going to be for a movie. Analysis such as this can end up needed in labeling the sentiment of the words used and even being part of a labeled data set. Resources for the sentiment of concepts and words will be made for concept net and word net.

The text is going to be used to catch emotions in affective computing. The text will be based on the various approaches that affective computing has used in things like news stories and student evaluations.

Academic applications

One of the issues for text mining is how important it is to publishers who have a large database of information that needs to be indexed. This is going to be especially true when it comes to scientific disciplines where there are highly specific pieces of information inside of the text. So, initiatives are going to be taken like nature's proposal for an interface that allows for open text mining.

Some of the academic institutions that have become involved with text mining are:

1. The National center for text mining which was the first publicly funded text mining center in the entire world. This center is operated by the University of Manchester as well as the Tsujii lab from the University of Tokyo. These two collectives are creating customized tools and research facilities that are going to offer advice to the academic community.

They are funded by the joint information systems committee as well as the United Kingdom research councils. The main focus is on text mining inside of biomedical and biological sciences. However, the research continues to expand into areas like social sciences.
2. In the United States, you are going to find the school of information located at the University of California where a program is being developed called BioText so that biology researchers can use text mining and its analysis.
3. The text analysis portal for research is housed at the University of Alberta and has a scholarship project to work on the newest text analysis applications while creating a gateway for researchers who are new to the practice to be able to work with it.

Chapter 4: Data Management

Data management is going to be all of the disciplines that you use to manage data so that it is a valuable resource.

There is a foundation in Europe known as the European Foundation for Quality Management as well as the Competence Center Corporate Data Quality that says corporate data quality management is the complete set of activities that you are going to use to improve the quality of your data both preventive and reactive. One of the main premises for this is the business relevance of high-quality data at the corporate level. Some of the activities you may use for high-quality data will be.

1. Strategy for corporate data quality. Here different business drivers are going to be affected and there are going to be multiple divisions inside of an organization that work on it together. All

in all, every department in a company needs to work together to ensure that they are working with the highest quality of data.

2. Corporate data quality controlling. There has to be a strict policy to monitor the data according to the company's policies, standards, and procedures. Any changes in the compliance of the data should be reported to the stakeholders.

3. Corporate data quality organization will be where the roles and responsibilities are defined so that everyone knows what they are expected to do with the data that they are working with.

4. To handle the data properly and in a standardized way and to ensure the data quality, corporate data quality processes and methods are put into place throughout the entire company. Standard procedures and guidelines must be put into place in the company's daily processes.

5. Data architecture for corporate data quality. The architecture of the data is going to be the model that you are using which will be made up of the models that are used for corporate data and the storage of that data along with how it is distributed.
6. Applications for corporate data quality will include the software applications that are used to support the activities mentioned above. Any software that is used has to be monitored, managed, and improved upon continuously.

Data management is also going to be included in managing the databases that your data is being stored on. You will have to clean out the database and make sure that it has enough space on it to hold all of the data that you are working with. Not only that, you are also going to have to ensure that it has been updated and only those that need to get into the database have access to it. This is going to prevent people from getting a hold of data that they should not have access to.

Which leads us to the security of that data. You have to ensure that your data is protected completely due to the fact that you may be working with data that is sensitive. Take for example, if you are working in a doctor's office. The data that you are working with is going to consist of people's social security numbers, birthdays, and health issues. If someone was to get a hold of that, not only would they be able to steal someone's identity, but they could sell the information online.

Therefore, you have to make sure that you have passwords and that files are encrypted whenever they are sent between workers so that if it does fall into the wrong hands, it is not going to be easily accessed. Along with that, but you are going to know whenever someone tries to get the data because you will receive an alert that someone is trying to access it with the incorrect password.

Now, what do you do with data that you no longer need? The retention policy for your company is going to vary depending on where you work, but just because data is no longer needed does not mean that you can just delete it. There are going to be rules that you are going to have to follow in order to discard of the data in a safe way so that personal and confidential information that is listed in that data is not freely given to someone who may be going through the trash or gets your computer whenever you upgrade.

If you are working with paper then the best thing that you can do is mark out all of the data that no one needs to have and then shred it. You can do the same thing on your computer by placing a shredding program on the computer. You will need to speak to your company's IT department about this before you do it.

Managing your data is also going to include how you put it onto paper so that those who are using the data to make decisions can see it in an obvious way rather than having to try and locate what they are looking for. Below is one of the best ways that you can manage your data in an organized fashion not only for you but for those using it to make decisions that could affect your job.

Decision tree

Your decision tree will be the tool that you are going to use whenever you need support in the decisions that you are making. The decision tree is called a tree because it looks like a tree of your decisions and outcomes have been listed. This is another way that you can display algorithms that were used in the analysis process

Decision trees will be used when working with operations research, or more specifically, whenever the decision report that you do needs to identify the strategies that were used so that you could reach that goal. But, you are going to find it is more popular when dealing with machine learning.

When it comes time to think about the decision tree, you should think of it like a flow chart where all of the nodes and tests that are run can be placed so that you can show the result of each test. With decision analysis, the decision tree is going to be used as an influence diagram that you will apply when you are using visual tools for the values that you expect and any alternatives that have been collected.

Most of the decision trees that you work with are going to have at least three nodes.

1. End nodes: These are typically going to be triangles. These are the final result of that decision.
2. Decision nodes: The squares that are on your tree that are going to show choices that you can choose from.
3. Chance nodes: These nodes are going to be shown by circles on your tree. The chance nodes are the ones that show what happens if you take the path instead of a different one.

Your tree will be used in research that is done by operations along with management for those operations. Usually, the decisions are going to be online and there will not be any recall under the data that comes back as incomplete. Decision trees have to show the parallelism between probability models and the best choice for the algorithm that should be used inside of that model. You can also use a tree for calculating conditional probabilities.

Tree elements

When you look at a decision tree, you are going to read it left to right just like you would anything else. There are going to be burst nodes on the tree, but there will not be any sink nodes. So, when created manually, a tree can get enormous due to the fact that someone is manually drawing the tree and adding the nodes that need to be added.

Decision rules

A lot of decision trees will be linearized with rules of the decision so that your outcomes are in the left node and the conditions are going to follow will conjoin with an if clause. Your rules are usually going to come in this form.

If (condition 1) and (condition 2) and (condition 3) then (the outcome)

Your decision rules will be created by the rules of association where the variable for your target is listed on the right. Decision rules are also going to show temporal or causal relations on your tree.

Decision tree with symbols

You may find your decision tree looks a lot like a flow chart and contains symbols that are used in order to make it easier for the person making the decision to understand and read the data and make an informed decision

Rule induction

Decision trees can also be seen as generative models based on the rules that come from empirical data. These trees are going to be used in order to define the various accounts of data all while attempting to minimize the number of levels that are shown on the tree.

Chapter 5: Data Reduction and Clustering

Data reduction is known as the transformation of digital information derived empirically or experimentally into the corrected and most simple form possible. One of the basic concepts of reduction is to take the data down to the most meaningful parts.

Whenever information is pulled from readings off of a machine there is going to be a transformation period where it is taken from analog and placed into digital form. When the data is already in digital form, then the reduction is going to be when you go in and edit it so that you can create a tabular summary.

Whenever observations are kept discrete, then the underlying phenomenon is continuous then you are going to have to use interpolation and smoothing. Most of the time, data reduction is going to be used to find the measurement errors. There are some ideas that the errors are going to be needed before the value can be determined.

Take for example those who work in astronomy have to reduce the data from the satellites that are constantly recording data so that we can discover new worlds. If they did not reduce the data, then we would be going through thousands of megabytes of data which could cause us to miss out on learning something new.

There is even some research going on about reducing data that comes off of wireless devices that are used for monitoring health and making a diagnosis.

Reducing data may seem like a lot of work, but in the end, it is going to be helpful because you are going to be able to locate the data that you need to work with instead of trying to work with all of the data that is within your grasp. Not only that, but you are going to be reducing costs because you are only going to be working with the data that you absolutely need.

To top it off you are going to be doing your job more effectively since you are not going to be wasting your time with data that is useless, but you are going to be making yourself valuable to your boss because you are not going to be going to them with information that is going to place your project back. Instead, you will be presenting accurate data in a way that just leaves the decision-making process to them.

Reducing data is also going to assist you in getting rid of duplicate data that you are not going to need, therefore you are going to combine data so that it lessens the load of data that you are working with. Along with this, you are going to be opening up storage for more data which is going to make it to where you are not constant deleting data.

Whenever you reduce data, you will be able to see what is missing and if you really need to obtain that piece of data. Along those lines, when you are only getting the data that is missing, you are reducing your workload since you are not going to be having to redo your investigation going through and getting all of the data once more.

When it comes to creating visualizes having reduced data will make your visual smaller and easier to follow. This is going to make your life easier because you are not going to have to worry about trying to figure out how to present the data and how to make it to where people can follow the data in a way that they can understand it.

Another wonderful thing about reducing your data is that you are not going to have as many tests to run to prove your hypothesis.

Best practices

These are some of the most common techniques used for data reduction

1. Order the data by size
2. Give a brief summary of the data
3. Table diagonalization where all of the rows and columns for the table is reorganized to make the patterns easier to discover.
4. Take out the chart junk like pictures and extra lines
5. Round to at least one or two of the most effective digits. The effective digits are going to be the ones that vary as part of the data that is being used.
6. Use a layout that is easy to follow and labels so that the person looking at the chart knows where to look next.
7. Use averages in order to provide a visual focus just like the summary.

Data clustering

Clustering is the task of grouping objects in a way that they fall into the same group. These objects are going to be similar in nature. The main task for exploratory data mining and statistical data analysis is to use things like image analysis, information retrieval so on and so forth.

Cluster analysis is not going to work on one specific algorithm, but the general task is going to end up being solved through various algorithms that are going to differ in their notion of what constitutes a cluster and exactly how efficient it is.

There are some popular notions for clusters that are going to include small distances that fall between the cluster members and dense area of data space. Clustering is going to be formulated as a multi objective optimization problem. There is going to be an appropriate clustering algorithm along with parameter settings which are going to depend on the individual data sets and how the results are going to be used.

Connectivity based clustering

This clustering method is going to also be known as hierarchical clustering which is going to be based on the core idea of the objects being related to objects that are nearby than objects that are further apart. With this algorithm, the objects are going to be connected to create clusters based on how far apart they are. Clusters are going to be described the maximum distance needed to connect the parts of the cluster.

Centroid based clustering

With this algorithm, the clusters will be represented by a central vector that is not going to necessarily be a member of that data set. Whenever the number of clusters is fixed to k. k is going to be defined as an optimization problem where you will find k cluster centers and then assign those objects to the nearest cluster center which is going to square the distances from the cluster so they are minimized.

The approach of NP-hard, which is the known optimization problem, is going to search for the approximate solutions. This is often referred to as the k means algorithm, and also known as Lloyd's algorithm method.

Distribution based clustering

In this clustering model, it is going to be related to the statistics that you find in distribution models. The objects that belong to the same distribution are known as clusters. Resembling the way that artificial data sets are generated through a random sampling of objects from the distribution is one of the convenient properties of this approach.

As this is a theoretical foundation of the model, they are going to suffer from the problem of over fitting unless you put constraints on the model's complexity. The more complex that the model is, the better the data will be explained.

Data based clustering

The clusters are going to be described as the areas that are made of higher density than those left over in the data set with density based clustering. Separate clusters are going to be required by the objects inside of the sparse areas; they are usually treated to be border points and noise.

DBSCAN is known as one of the more common density based clustering methods. There are some newer methods that are going to be defined as density reachability. Some are similarly linked to based clustering which is based on the connecting of points that are inside of some certain distance points. But, it is only connecting points, that are going to satisfy the density criterion that was stated in the original variant as defined by the least number of other objects that sit inside of the radius. The cluster is going to be consistent with all the density connected objects as well as the objects that are inside of that object's range.

Another property of the DBSCAN is going to be that it is not as complex as you may think it would be. It is going to require a linear number of ranged queries that are in the database and it is going to be discovered with the same results.

The biggest drawback to DBSCAN is going to be that it will expect a density drop in order to detect the cluster borders. On most data sets, there is going to be some overlapping Gaussian distributions which are going to be a common use when it comes to artificial data. The clusters borders are going to be produced by the algorithms.

Other Recommended Books

Machine Learning

LINK: http://amzn.to/2xCDN19

Markov Models

LINK: http://amzn.to/2ey04bI

Chapter 6: Web Scraping

When you scrape data that will be utilized for the obtaining data from websites, that is called as web scraping. By searching in a web browser or by using hypertext transfer protocol, web scraping software can be found. As you web scrap, it will have to be done manually by the user of the software. In other words, you will be copying text off of the internet and place it into a database or spreadsheet for analysis or retrieval at a later date.

Web scraping on a web page means that you are going to be calling the web page and then pulling information from it. The fetching of a page means that you are going to be downloading it which your computer browser is going to do whenever you are viewing it. Once that is done, web crawling will be used as the main component for web scraping in which you are going to fetch pages to process later.

After the fetching is completed, then the extraction process is going to take place. The page's content will be searched and modified as the data is copied over to a spreadsheet.

Web scraping is going to usually start by taking something off of a web page in order to use it somewhere else, for instance, you would be taking phone numbers and name of companies that you are going to call later.

Techniques

Web scraping is a process that is going to occur automatically whenever you are mining data. The only thing is that you are going to be getting everything off of the internet exclusively. Most of the time it is going to be the interactions between humans and computers. All of the current web scraping solutions are going to range from humans taking care of the scraping to systems being automated in able to convert an entire website into a structured information that has limitations.

Human copy and paste

There are going to be times that the best web scraping technology is not going to be good enough to do what it is that you are wanting to do, therefore it makes a human's manual examination the best solution. Not just that, but there are times that this is going to be the only solution whenever there are barriers set up by websites to stop machine automation.

Text pattern matching

Another easy but equally as effective approach in getting data from a web page is to use the UNIX grep command to find patterns while facilitating programming languages such as Python or Perl.

HTTP programming

The web pages that are static or dynamic can be pulled through the posting of HTTP requests through the remote web server by using socket programming.

HTML parsing

There are a lot of websites that have an enormous collection of pages that are generated dynamically with an underlying structured source such as a database. The data is going to be in the same category and is usually going to be encoded through similar pages by a common template or script.

When data mining, the program is going to detect a template from the proper information source to pull the content and then translate it into a more relational form known as the wrapper.

The wrapper is going to create algorithms that are going to assume the input pages for the wrapper will induction systems so it can conform to the template that they identified in turns of the URL's common scheme.

DOM parsing

Whenever a website is embedded in a web browser like Mozilla Firefox, the browser control will determine on if the program can retrieve the dynamic content that is generated on the client side of the script.

Browsers such as these are going to control the parse web pages inside of a DOM tree which is going to be based on the programs that are used to retrieve parts of the web pages.

Vertical aggregation

There are a few companies that are developing vertical specific harvesting platforms. These platforms are going to be used to create and monitor the massive number of bots that are being used for specific verticals inside of the no man in the loop – there is no direct human involvement – which means that there is no work related to the targeted site.

There is some preparation involved which is going to mean that you have to establish a knowledge base for the entire vertical and then the platform will end up creating a lot to do the work for you.

Semantic annotation recognizing

There are pages that you may scrap that will embrace the metadata, the semantic markups, and the annotations in order to locate specific pieces of data. Should the annotations be embedded in the pages like Microformat does, then this technique is going to be seen as a special case for the DOM parsing.

In other words, the annotations are going to be organized, stored, and managed apart from the web pages in order for you to obtain the data before the page is scraped.

Computer version web page analysis

There are going to be some efforts that are going to use machine learning as well as computer versions in order to try and identify the exact information from web pages through the interpretation of the page like a human may do.

Software

The software tools that are made available for you to web scrap can be customized for the web scraping solutions that you need. It is this software that will attempt to automatically figure out the data structure for the page or provide the recording interface that is going to remove the necessity that is there to manually write out the web scraping code or other scripting functions that are going to be used to extract and transform the content in the databases interface that will end up being stored in a database.

There are some web scraping software that will be used in order to extract data from the API.

Some examples of the tools that you may use are:

1. URL is a command line tool that contains a library that can be used to transfer the data inside of a URL to support a wide range of http methods such as GET and POST.
2. Diffbot will use a computer version to automatically extract the data from a web page through the interpretation of pages visually just like a human would.

3. Data toolbar is an add on that you can use with web browsers such as Google Chrome, Mozilla Firefox, and Internet Explorer to collect data that is structured from that web page and convert it into a tabular format that will then be entered into a database or spreadsheet.
4. Heritrix will obtain the pages and then use a web crawler to design a web archiving that is written by the internet archive.
5. HTML unit will take a headless browser so that it can retrieve web pages for web scraping and more.
6. Imacros is an extension for the browser that you use in order to record code, share it, and replay the browser automation.

JavaScript

1. jQuery
2. Grease monkey
3. Node.js
4. phantomJS

SaaS version

1. fscraper
2. import.io
3. uScraper

Web crawling framework

This framework is going to be used in order to build web scrapers that you are going to have the option of using. If this is the option that you are wanting, then you will use Scrapy.

Preventing web scraping

There are tools that the administrators of websites can use to slow down or even stop bots from scraping their website.

1. Block IP address. This can be done manually or based on criteria that you set up for your website like geolocation and DNSRBL. In doing this you are going to be blocking all of the devices that browser from that IP address.
2. Disable the web services API so that the website's system is not exposed.
3. There are some bots that are going to say who they are through user agent strings. You have the option of blocking based on this such as robots that use text like google bot. There are other bots that are going to not make a distinction between them or a human that is using the browser so it may be harder to tell

the difference so that you can block them.

4. Bots can be blocked through the monitoring of excessive traffic that your web page sees.
5. There are some bots that are going to be easier to be blocked with the tools that you are using due to the fact that you can make it to where you can verify if a real person is using the site through Captchas. Bots are not always going to be coded to get past some of the captcha patterns or they may even employ a third-party service to get a human to get past the captcha challenges before taking over once more. This is how some sites are scraped despite the fact that they use devices to stop bots.

Chapter 7: Data Analysis in the Real World

There are risks that you have to know about in order to be able to do data analytics properly in order to protect yourself, your company, and your data.

1. Data security

Security is going to be the first thing that anyone thinks of when it comes to dealing with businesses and people who are working with data. They are not going to want another company to get a hold of data that they can use to bet you out on something new that you are trying to put out. At the point in time that data is taken from a big company, it makes news and is not forgotten due to the fact that it opens the public's eyes to how easily other people can get a hold of their data. The more data that a company has, the bigger target they make themselves.

2. Data privacy

It is not going to matter what type of data is being used, it has to be protected and the privacy should be kept to those who absolutely need to know about the information. The less information that is told to those who do not need to know it, the less risk you are going to be opening yourself up to.

3. Costs

There are going to be costs that are going to be associated with the collection of data, however, there are also going to be costs for storing and analyzing the data as well. Then you have to throw in the compliance costs that you will have to pay so that you can avoid issues that are going to be associated with your data.

It is at this point that you are going to need to get rid of data that is not needed so that you can save some money and time not having to go through unnecessary procedures.

4. Bad analytics

This occurs whenever you misinterpret the data that you are analyzing. In the event that you draw links between the various parts of data is going to be a coincidence. The data that you work with from something big, you are going to be able to draw some links, but that does not mean that the links that you can draw are going to be correct.

5. Bad data

Sometimes there will be a collection of data that is not going to be worth anything. Bad data is collected when you do not have enough time to gather the appropriate data for the study that you are conducting. This can hurt your company due to the fact that you are going to have to take the time once again to get a hold of the data that you need or you will have to put out a product without the proper data which can harm sales in your company.

Real world examples

You can easily say that data analysis happens in the real world, but how are you going to know what to look for if you do not have a few examples. In this section, we are going to discuss how you can spot real world examples of the data analysis.

Video streaming services

When it comes to video streaming services you can watch entire videos online without having to wait for the next episode to air. But, the service is collecting data from you as you watch.

Depending on what you are watching and how you rate them is going to tell the service what recommendations it should give you thanks to the data that it is analyzing. This also helps to tell them what to keep on their site and off their site.

Ancestors

Some websites allow for you to find out more about your family all by placing a few facts about yourself and your family into the website. The more information that you want, the more information that you are going to have to put in.

The data that you place into their system is going to be sent out the database and analyzed in order to match it up with other records that have data that you are looking for. The data is going to be analyzed carefully in order to make sure that you are not paired up with incorrect family records.

Medical research

Medical research is not always going to occur on a human being. There are times that it is going to happen on a strain of bacteria as the doctor doing the research is attempting to figure out how to cure a disease or figure out how to knock out something like the common cold.

This data is going to be extracted from the study and analyzed to see if it works or not. If it does not work then they are going to continue with their research.

One example is the study of the E. Coli strain to see if the doctor could figure out how to kill the strain with the proper mix of antibiotics.

Weather

There is an independent system operator that you can find in California that helps over thirty-five million customers get their power. The software that the ISO uses is going to collect data points to ensure that the power is still on and look at weather so that if the power goes out, they can work to get it fixed as fast as possible.

This is also going to be similar to a water company in Ontario that provides water for residences and businesses.

Infusion pumps

It is important to know that when it comes to infusions, doctors and nurses do not need to go chasing an infusion pump down when they need it. There is software being used in one hospital that keeps track of how the patient is doing on their infusion which assists the doctor in figuring out if the infusion is working for the patient or not.

Vegas

The machines that you see in Vegas are going to collect data. If there are not many people playing that slot machine, then that machine is taken out and another is put in its place. This is done so that their profits continue to go through the roof.

Conducting data analysis

Here is where you are going to get a more broken-down version of what data analysis truly is.

Organize your data

1. When using an electronic database, you need to organize your data. Whenever placing this data in the database, you have to make sure that all of the data is going to the proper place. There are applications such as excel that you can use in order to organize the data in a spreadsheet that will enable you to search the data quickly.
2. Put your responses into digital form. If you have conducted a survey, then you will take the answers to that survey and count them out so that you can look at how many answered that question that specific way.
3. You are going to organize your data by age or gender depending on how it best works for that study.
4. Check for mistakes, you do not want your work to be filled with mistakes or else your work is not going to be accurate.

Statistical tests

1. T tests are some of the most common tests that are going to be run on the data that you are working in order to find the average of the samples that have been collected.
2. You can also run an ANOVA test to compare the means of multiple groups. This is a powerful test to find out the differences in your comparisons.
3. Linear regression is going to help you to see the variances depending on what the dependent variable is. Whenever you use linear regression, you will be measuring the association between two variables and how clear the connection is.
4. Your ANCOVA test can be used by taking two regression lines and comparing them such as ages or genders.

Analyzing the data

1. Ensure that your question is defined. You are not going to want a study question that is impossible to answer.
2. Talk to a statistician to get their help with the statistics. Working with statistics can be hard and the more data that you are working with, the more complex it is going to be. However, a statistician is going to be able to analyze the data and tell you exactly which tests to run in order to get you the results that you are wanting. They also can look at the data after it has been collected and let you know if it was tested properly or not.
3. Pick the statistical test that you are wanting to run and run it. You will need to find some program like SAS or R that you can use to execute the test. So, keep

in mind that if you use a program, you are going to need some programming experience to make sure that you are running the test properly.

Chapter 8: Social Network Analysis

The process that you use in order to investigate the social structures through the use of networks and graph theory is called social network analysis. Through social network analysis, the network structures in terms of nodes that are connected to them are going to be characterized. Some examples would be to visualize social media networks, friendships, and sexual relationships. Social network analysis came up as a method to modern sociology and has acquired a compelling following in other studies.

Metrics

Homophily is going to extend to which actors will form times with those that are similar versus the dissimilar ones. Similarities are going to be defined by race and age. This is also referred to assortativity.

The number of content forms that are contained inside of a tie will be shown by multiplexity. For instance, two people who are working together but they are friends which give them a multiplexity of two.

Mutuality/reciprocity the extent is going to show how two actors are going to interact with each other.

Propinquity is the tendency for actors to have ties that are geographically close to others.

Network closure is the measure of completeness for relational triads such as a person's friends who are friends with those friends. This would be called a transitivity.

Distributions

An individual's weak ties that will fill a structural hole which is going to provide a link between two people is known as the bridge. It is also going to be the shortest route whenever the longer one is not possible because of the elevated risk of distortion.

Density is the portion of direct ties inside of the network which relates to the total number possible.

Centrality will refer to a group of metrics that is going to quantify the importance of a node inside of the network.

Distance is the least amount of ties that is required between two people.

Tie strength will define the linear combination of reciprocity, intimacy, and time. The stronger the ties are associated to propinquity, transitivity, and homophily. The weaker ties are tied to the bridges.

Structural holes show the absence of ties between two distinct parts of a network. You will be able to find and exploit the structural holes that can give someone a competitive advantage. This concept is often referred to as the alternative conception of social capital and was developed by an American sociologist, Ronald Burt.

Segmentation

The groups are going to be called cliques in which each person is tied to directly. These social circles are going to be less stringency of direct contact which is going to imprecise the blocks in the event that precision is wanted.

Clustering coefficients are going to be the measure of the likelihood of two associated nodes. The higher the clustering coefficient will indicate the greater cliquishness.

The degree in which people are connected directly to each other by cohesive bonds will be shown by cohesion. The structural cohesion is going to relate to the least number of people who would be considered to be disconnected from the group.

Models and visualization

When it comes to the network data, it is necessary to know about the visual representation of the social network and it will show you the results of the analysis. There are many methods that you can use to show the data that is obtained by social network analysis. Modules that you can use for network visualization can be found in most of the analytic software.

Exploration of the data will be made by the displaying nodes and tie into other layouts while attributing to size, color, and other properties that you are going to find out about the nodes. The visual representations of the networks are going to be powerful methods used for conveying the complexity of the information, however, it will end up to misrepresenting the structural properties in order to capture a quantitative analysis if interpreting the node and the graph's properties for the visual displays alone will not be done carefully.

There are signed graphs that are going to show you both the good and the bad relationships that occur between humans. One of the positive edges is between two nodes will denote a positive relationship while the negative between the nodes is going to show you the negative in a relationship.

Signed social networks are going to have unbalanced and balanced cycles. Balanced cycles are going to be cycles where the products are positive. A group of people who probably are not going to change their opinions about the other people in the group are going to be represented by the balanced graphs according to a balanced theory.

A group of people who are going to change their opinion of those in the group will be shown in unbalanced graphs.

Social network analysis will be used as a tool to facilitate change by showing different approaches of participatory network mapping. Those that participate in your study are going to give you the data that you need to map out a network as you conduct your study. One example of this is to take a pen and paper to your session and show how each person is perceived through influences and goals that they have in their careers.

Being able to collect qualitative data and then figure out how to ask clear questions all the while making sure that the network data is collected properly is one benefit that you are going to discover.

Networking potential

Social networking potential is going to be a numeric coefficient that is derived through the use of algorithms. To represent the size of someone's social network and how they can influence that network, these algorithms are going to be used. There are two primary functions for the social networking potential coefficients.

1. How people are classified based on their social networking potentials.
2. The weights of the respondents in quantitative marketing research studies

When you calculate the social network potential of those that are in your study, you can target high social networking potential respondents as well as the relevance and strength of the marketing research that is going to drive the viral marketing strategies to be improved.

Variables can be used to determine a person's social networking potential which is going to include those who are participating, their activities, group memberships, recognition, leadership roles, and how they contribute to non- electronic media as well as the past distribution of information inside of their network.

The acronym for social networking potential as well as the first algorithms that were developed to help quantify to a person's social networking potential was first described in the white paper "Advertising Research is Changing" which was published in 2003.

The very first book was written to discuss how Alpha users work among mobile telecoms audiences according to 3G marketing by Ahonen Kasper and Melkko in '04.

Practical applications

Social network analysis can be utilized thoroughly in a great extent of disciplines and applications. There are some common network applications which include mining, data aggregation, network modeling, network propagation, network modeling, behavior analysis and sampling.

Businesses in the private sector use the social network to support activities like analysis and customer interactions, marketing demands and business intelligence. There are some public sectors that are using it as well in order to develop leader engagement strategies to analyze the community-based problem solving and group or individual engagement for media use.

The social network analysis will also be used for intelligence activities. Techniques such as this are going to allow for the analysts to map an undercover or underground organization like an intelligence ring or a street gang. The NSA uses it to do analysis tests on terrorist cells or other networks that seem like they are a threat to national security.

So, in other words, social network analysis is going to show you the relationships that you are going to find between people. This does not have to be how they put their personal life out on social media, but how they work together. There is no escaping the negative relationships because they are a part of life, but they can be used to analyze and figure out how to prevent those negative relationships from happening to other people.

The positive relationships are going to be used to figure out how you can promote other healthy and positive relationships amongst people which are going to help create those positive ties with other people.

These ties are going to show you how other people tie to each other in such a way that you are going to be able to figure out how everyone works together in the world and how human interaction is important.

Chapter 9: Data Analysis Techniques

1. Develop the questions that need to be researched and link them to a study that you are able to design

Data is going to be collected to answer a question. The question should be able to answer a question in a way that it can be tested in a study so that you can take the data that you collect and analyze it in order to make sure you make your boss and customer happy.

These studies are going to answer questions or be experiments that you can conduct. The case studies will give you a plethora of information that is going to assist in making you company go further in a more productive manner. You should keep these three things in mind when it comes to your question.

a. Is your question well-articulated?
b. Is your question able to be answered with the resources and time limit that you are working against?
c. Is your question a good fit with the study that you are conducting?

Whenever you are planning the research that you are going to be doing, you are going to want to ensure that you have a clear purpose as to what it is that you are trying to accomplish and the questions we listed above are going to help make sure that happens.

You are going to want to discover a few different study objectives to show you a variety of data for you to analyze.

You will want to collect and analyze the qualitative data that has been collected.

Four different uses for collecting data are:
1. Individual interviews: these are going to be discussions that occur between at least two different people and are going to have some sort of structure to them as well as a purpose that is trying to be met. The interviewer is going to be trying to get any knowledge or perspective that the interviewee has on the topic that is being investigated. This is usually done in an effort to get additional facts from that individual to learn more about the topic that is at hand.
2. Focus group discussions: focus groups are typically groups that are organized and are going to consist of six to eight different people discussing the topic that is being researched. As the people

discuss the issue at hand, they are going to be able to agree and disagree with each other and the opinions that are being put before them to address based on their own beliefs and experiences. The people that you choose for the focus group need to be relevant to what it is that you are trying to study and make sure that you inform the participants about everything that they are going to be discussing. You will want to recruit people that are going to give you a good representation of the population that you are targeting.

3. Photo voice: this method is going to allow for a person to identify and help improve their community, life, or engage in a program through the use of photography and captions that go with that photograph. Photo voice is going to enable the group of people participating to have access to a camera that is going to allow them to discuss and share

stories that are going to be significant to what you are studying.

4. Picture story: This method is going to be aimed mostly at children so that they are able to participate in the study in a fun way that is going to be geared towards their learning level. These pictures are going to be pictures that they draw or stories that they tell depending on how old they are and where their level of literacy lies. This is typically an inexpensive research method that is going to get the views of the child on what they are being asked.

When it comes to the samples of those that may participate in your study, you are going to use at least one of these methods.

1. Random purposeful sampling: this sampling is going to be purposeful, and

the group will be primarily made up of random participants.

2. Extreme or typical sampling: you will learn about the strange or the standard tests such as those who have gone through the struggle that you are studying.

3. Snowball sampling: you will ask multiple people to point out others who can be interviewed as well due to the fact that they are open and contain some kind of understanding of the issue you are studying.

2. Qualitative data analysis

The data analysis is going to be whenever you take the data that has been collected reduced down to the amounts that make sense while ensuring that you have something from all of the sources that have participated in your study. The impressions that are gathered will shed light and answer the question that you wanted to answer.

Using this process means that you are going to be taking the information that is the most descriptive information to find out the explanation or interpretation of what information you have gathered.

Just like was discussed earlier, you are going to want to make sure that you are cleaning up your data so that you do not have to worry about working with data that is not useful or is going to negate your research.

Qualitative analysis will end up paying special attention to the words that come out of people's mouths so that you can attempt to figure out if there is any contradiction to the research or to show a theme or trend that can emerge from the data that you have collected.

When it comes to analyzing your data, you will have to reduce the data to the data that only falls inside of the framework so that they can help you get to your object, all while falling inside of the policy that was set into place when you first formed your question.

When it comes to reducing your data, you will be looking for answers that keep to the topic of your question that you are attempting to answer. This is going to be the cleaning process that was discussed earlier in the book.

Many in data analysis recommend that you take a more exploratory perspective in order to look at any new impressions that are going to assist in shaping your interpretation and finding things that you did not see before. While you code your data, you are going to see some abstract themes most likely that are going to appear in the data that has been coded. You are going to also see links between the codes that have been created which is going to bring out more information that will hopefully support your research question.

There are some codes that are not going to have anything to do with what it is that you are researching which are going to help you either drop or tie the data into a common theme. The common themes are going to be open to the organized theme that you are working on which then is going to lead to one global theme. The global theme tied to your analysis will usually show an illustration of the research that you did to answer the question that you started studying.

3. Methods for your quantitative data

When you have collected data, there will be some typical forms that you are going to see in your data.

- Scores or rankings
- Units

- Rates of change
- Pricing
- Percentages

The analysis that is done will be used to create a summary of the numerical data for a visualization aid like a chart or graph.

Most of the quantitative data that is obtained will come in a wide variety of forms based on the sources that were used in your research.

- Services offered by a provider or the assessments done at a facility: these are often carried out whenever the participants are under supervision.
- Surveys and questionnaires: these methods are typically going to have questions that are constructed based on a ranking system where the answers are scored. The questions may also be close-ended questions where the respondent

is limited to a certain number of answers that they can choose from.

- The service provider or data from a facility: you can pull data from a health care clinic such as records for the children that were vaccinated or from a school of their attendance for that week.
- Biophysical measurements: things such as height and weight.
- Project records: these are going to be some of the best resources for data. These files are going to be things such as a training event that a school holds and how many people actually attend.

BONUS - Business Intelligence

In this bonus chapter you will learn valuable insights and priceless info. This chapter in particular will be especially beneficial to those current or future business owners and potential entrepreneurs alike. Whether you are in the preliminary stages of planning your business or at launch stage, the information contained within this chapter will greatly aid you and perhaps even open your eye to new opportunities you may have not seen before. Let's get to it.

Business intelligences encompasses a wide range of factors such as discerning markets, laws, accounting and management. First off when we discuss business, and I mean any kind of business we must address two fundamental elements. *Mindset* and *Systems*. Now this may not sound like a secret formula to make a fortune, but hear me out. In order to operate any successful business, we need to get our mindset right, and in particular the way we think must take a drastic shift from employee to owner mentality. Meaning we want to "work on our business" and "not work in your business". Understand the differences, working in your business connotes your caught up internally and actually work like any other employee. Working on your business takes more of an ownership role, and although you do not directly engage in the business, however you control it from afar and make crucial decisions.

One's perception about money tells you a lot. I'll elaborate, employees work for money, but business owners make money work for them.

We need to get down to the psychology of money, and in reality money is just an illusion, and in essence we give money value as a medium or vehicle in which we engage in commerce. Employees think " how can I work to get more money?", and look for opportunities with benefits and job security. Business owners think " How can I make money work for me?", and exponentially make it grow. There are clear and distinct differences between both perceptions, and obviously one is definitely more favorable than the other.

Moving on to "systems". Earlier I discussed setting your mindset in the right way and making a drastic shift from employee to owner mentality. Now we must discuss systems and how to properly leverage systems found within businesses. Do you recall when I mentioned the phrase " make money work for you", I am referring to having systems in place that generates revenue for you consistently and on a perpetual basis. If you wanted to learn how to play basketball, how would you go about doing this? You would most likely need to learn the body mechanics involved, rules and regulations, interact with your teammates, practice drills, get coaching and learn gameplay strategies. What I just described here was a system, and this system would teach you the ins and outs of the game of basketball from beginning to end.

Now how does this translate into real world business? Well, much in the same way, I'll elaborate.

In order to run a business you need to have mechanisms, techniques/strategies, employees, and colleagues in place. First off, we would need to establish and define what our market is and if there is a demand for it. Secondly, we would need to outsource work to suppliers, assuming this is a retail business. Once we've established a chosen product, market and a reliable supplier we are ready to go to the next phase.

The very backbone for any business is marketing and sales . You would need to learn marketing or hire someone who knows how to market your product or services to a specific target audience. Honing your marketing capacities is essential for the survival of any business, and especially in this digital age where there are so many platforms in which you can leverage marketing to your target demographics.

Next, you need allies meaning build strong rapport with highly intelligent professionals, such as accountants and lawyers. Ask for their advice and insights and you would be surprised at how much progress you can make when you put more minds together. The purpose of having these professionals is to help you navigate through complex regulations, frameworks and legal jargon that you may have no knowledge of. Once this is all done you can start looking to hire reliable employees/managers to work for you. This part is just as crucial as any other component of the business model because a good employee can make or break your business too. This in essence is how you run a retail business, and once you have a system solidified in place you can expect recurring income that is essentially automatic. The initial start up phase will always be the hardest and take the most effort, but once things start to fall in place gradually you will be able to "make money work for you".

Different Types of Investments/ Businesses Models

In this sub chapter I'd like to discuss different types of investments and business models. First, let's talk about investing. When I say investing what is the first thing that comes to mind? Perhaps real estate, stocks, and bonds? Well, yes those are definitely investments depending on the circumstance. Before I go into detail about investing I'd like to discuss a crucial point, and that's knowing the differences between assets and liabilities. The reason why I am doing this is because before you may even start to think about making investments you need to ensure you have a proper understanding of assets and liabilities.

Whether you believe it or not, the vast majority of society does not really understand the distinct differences between an asset and liability. There is a reason why the growing gap between the poor and rich continually increases and this is due to lack of financial literacy. The poor tend to spend their hard earned dollars on depreciating assets or liabilities, while the rich invest their money into asset generating income. For instance, imagine someone wins a small fortune from the lottery. Perhaps 25 grand what do you think a poor person would do versus a rich person? Most likely spend it on a new car, designer clothes, expensive dinners and maybe even jewelry. Now these luxuries are nice and I have nothing against them if its within your means to afford it. However, upon further inspection we can see this person just squandered his money. I'll explain, as soon as you purchase a vehicle and step foot into it, the initial value has already decreased. Did you know when you step foot into a brand new car and use it for the first time, it has already depreciated by 5%-10% of its original value. Than generally speaking it depreciates at the rate of 15%-20% per year subsequently.

Now let's take a look at what a rich person would do with 25k. He or she would most likely look to invest in stocks, perhaps platinum, oil, and even cryptocurrencies like bitcoin. Speaking of which, if you want to learn about bitcoins and how to invest in them I would totally recommend you read the following book written by Raymond Kazuya, "Bitcoin & Cryptocurrencies Guide". Please see link below.

Link: http://amzn.to/2tRQpyj

A rich person would also probably start a business with the 25k. He or she would study markets and trends and from that information draw out a business plan and execute.

Remember the rich rent luxuries and spend on assets that generate income, but the poor only spend to own liabilities and do not invest in assets. Can you see the polar opposite mindsets and habits? The rich make every effort to stay rich and are in it for the long haul, but the poor only attempt to look rich and slowly deteriorate. Thus, the importance of having a good financial literacy and understanding of money, assets, and liabilities before you start investing.

It's time to look into different types of online business models. I personally chosen the most practical and easiest entry points which are online business models people can get into. Almost anyone can get into these types of ventures with very little start up costs.

***Affiliate Marketing* -** This business model is one of my favorites as you don't deal with inventory or have to create a product. It's all online, and you take a product that already exists and push it to the consumer, and when you make a sale you get a percentage of commission for that product sold. This is a very scalable business model, but you do have to be a little tech savvy, and understand the fundamentals of marketing, and how to effectively find your target audiences. My advice is if you get into this type of business model aim high and go hard. Meaning you need to push "high ticket products" in order to be extremely successful. There are both sides of the story to this low ticket and high ticket paradigm, and yes you can still making quite a substantial amount of money off the low ticket products, but why choose quantity over quality? See below the difference between high and low ticket products (Quality vs Quantity)

Low ticket product (quantity) - these products are generally below $100 and someone using these tactics is depending on quantity of products sold in order to generate a substantial amount of revenue. The good thing is affordable products equates to more sales, however the downside is the commission you make off it and the number of sales you need to make a decent living. So when you're doing product launches its more work for you in the long run and could potentially drain you. Also up selling will have a very low conversion rate for low end products and this is just the nature of the clientele.

High ticket product (quality) - These products are on the higher end $500+ and although it is quite the price tag for the average person you need to look at the long run. This type of demographic is extremely valuable and a lot easier to up sell too. They are more likely to convert and buy other related products and are simply more receptive to new deals, offers and bargins.

Now let's compare and contrast both high and low ticket products. Now let's say you make 15% per commission off a product, how much do you think you can make off a low end product? So for instance you sell a $9 product, and this equates to a $1.35 commission per sale, these are peanuts. Versus a $500 product sold at 15% commission which equates to a $75 commission per sale. Now this is not a fortune but, its far greater than its counterpart. If you took the low ticket product route at a $1.35 commission you would need 56 sales to catch up to 1 high ticket product sale!

The difference is vast and the better choice is obvious. With high ticket products you are engaging high quality customers, and let's face it generally speaking customers who are only willing to spend money on low end products will not make you rich! Also after taxes with $1.35 you're not really left with much. The point here is QUALITY over QUANTITY.

Drop shipping/Private Labeling - These business models are a bit more advanced and can get complicated. Let's start off by discussing drop shipping, what is drop shipping? You essentially own an online store (website) and you sell any product you want. You find a supplier through sites like Alibaba, Aliexpress, Global sources, Trade key, etc. - Do your own research before attempting to use any of these mentioned sites. You want to decide what type of product you will be selling and once you find a reliable supplier you fulfill an order through them and buy your products in bulk, which then gets shipped to a fulfillment center, which stores your items awaiting to be delivered to your customers.

There are fees associated with delivery and storage, so these must be taken into account for costs when deciding your selling price. The product you buy will most likely range from $1-$10 each. Thus, you want to mark up the price so you make a tidy profit. Dropping shipping operates similarly to any retail store, except you don't deal with inventory. Key considerations to remember; where are you purchasing from? -Who is your supplier? How long will products take to be shipped? - Usually if it's from China your waiting anywhere between 4-8 weeks and sometimes more! This can be an extremely stressful, and expect delays and perhaps even mismatched products sent to your customer. Customers WILL get impatient, so if you know a certain product will take long to arrive, don't take chances. The last thing you want is an angry customer who leaves a 1 star review, which can potentially destroy your business.

Speaking of reviews, you will need to set a budget aside for FREE promo launches and give your products out for free so some customers can potentially give you reviews. - This is also an essential component and crucial to ranking your product and will dictate the longevity of its selling rate and survival of your business.

Lastly advertising, you will need to learn how to leverage marketing tools such as Facebook to target specific audiences for your products. There are various resources on the internet that show you how to use Facebook ads. You essentially want to narrow down your demographics from gender, interests, and geographical location. The more specific the better in this line of business, wide range shot gun approaches are not necessarily the best thing to do! If you're like most people and have a limited budget you would just be burning your hard earned dollars.

So this was the gist of drop shipping and it can be quite a strenuous effort and big investment upfront. But if you master this business model and do get good at it your looking anywhere between **50,000 - 150,000** revenue at a 35% profit margin per month, which equates to roughly **19,000 - 52,000** net profit per month! That's after all your expenses on advertising, product purchase, shipping and storage costs. That's easily a six figure business all done at the click of a few buttons at the comfort of your home. - Note: It takes a lot of work and is not as easy as pushing a few buttons here and there. Stay away from hefty items and electronics as there are a lot of things that can go wrong with these types of products. Heavy items will incur you excess costs due to weight for shipping, and electronics can easily break from oversee travels, thus rendering damaged goods and refunded items, which is a double whammy to your business expenses.

Private Labeling - This business model is an interesting one in particular. You must first define your parameters, market, product and demographics. You will than select a product online, and ensure its a product that is not patented! Aim for products that will cost you between $10-$50 when starting out as you want to keep expenses low and mitigate any other potential pitfalls down the road, such as damaged goods or returned products from unsatisfied customers. Once you've selected a product you are ready for the next step.

Let's use a yoga mat for example as the selected product. Similar to drop shipping you will be utilizing fulfillment storage centers, and you want to aim for products under 5lb, remember the heavier the product the more you will be charged for delivery! Also, my advice is until you hone your talents and master this business model do not do electronic items. Now you have a chosen product it's time to contact your supplier or manufacturer, and you ask them to attach your own company logo to the desired product. (assuming you have a company)

Now you have a product with a brand that you OWN. Similar to drop shipping you will need to market, get reviews through give aways, do FREE promos and product launches. You will need to assess the competition and compete with people within your budget and league. Look for low competition and search for specific market niches.

High Level Corporate Marketing Consulting - This is one of my favorite models and is an advanced one. You really got to know your stuff, niches, and have ample marketing experience, intimately know your clientele and have brand presence. What does a corporate marketing consultant do? Your job is essentially to drive more sales, revenue and business growth for a company that contracts your marketing expertise and services. This is where your marketing skills would shine and you would use various marketing tools, platforms, SEO strategies, etc.

You must have a professional appearance, demeanor and a website that entails your services, and also having testimonial proofs of people who can vouch for you. Perhaps someone who can be a lead referral too. Considering the digital age we live in there are so many multi-million dollar companies getting left behind in marketing and the current digital trend. A lot of these "old school " and archaic companies do not know how to leverage the power of social media! It was Charles Darwin who said " It's not the strongest who survive, but it's those who are able to adapt". What happened to companies like Kodak (camera company that used film) ? they couldn't adapt and hop onto the trends fast enough. Digital cameras were the new hype, and this had a significant impact negatively on this film roll based photography company.

As a marketing consultant you are the agent or intermediary who is the sole driving force of generating revenue. You will utilize social media such as Facebook, Instagram, Twitter, and Pinterest. You will discover ways to increase efficiencies, sales, and drive massive traffic. A corporate consultant can make anywhere between ***10,000 - 50,000+*** per client! This could be over a 4 month, 6 month or even a 12 month period. Your aim as an online marketer is to produce long lasting results helping the company you have been contracted to work for reach the next stage of business and growth. The amount of work you get is dependent on your track record of success and if you can actually produce massive results. Again, this is strongly recommended for people who are extremely advanced in online marketing, tech savvy and who have strong work ethic.

Real Estate - Lastly I wanted to add one last business model, the real estate industry. Some consider it an indestructible industry and one of the most scalable. The reason I decided to mention this industry in the list of "online business models" is because a lot of skills overlap and are easily transferable. I want to keep your mind open for opportunities down the road. What is real estate? Without trying to complicate things and give you a convoluted definition, let's just say real estate is essentially selling "high ticket products".

Depending on what country, city or whatever geographical location you reside within regulations, rules and policies differ place to place. So it's up to you to be informed and do your own research and stay up to date. This is definitely a lucrative industry and perhaps one of the most competitive . But let's dissect some fundamentals of real estate, so you can better understand what it is. Earlier I discussed high ticket products and vouched for quality over quantity. Well guess what? Real estate operates on the same exact principles, and these "houses" is what you consider high ticket products.

Of course this is a highly regulated industry which contains many regulatory frameworks that are set in place that you must abide by and be aware of. Again, due to the nature and scope of this industry differing from country to country I cannot give you exact details as it will differ from one geographical location to another. But, the fundamentals are essentially the same to affiliate marketing. You find a market and a product that already exists, and in this case a house and the housing/condo industry. You push a the product and make a sale, and get a commission off it. Therefore, you get a house sold and earn a commission on it. Now this type of commission is far greater than 99% of affiliate marketing products you will be able to find.

You can consider this a top of the line commission. So how much can you make? Well, I'll give you an example. If you deal with a high value demographic and sell a 1.5 million dollar house at a low end **%2** commission you will receive a $30,000 commission for that one sale! That's more money than some people make in a year! Incredible right?

(0.02 x 1500000 = 30,000)

Business Intelligence Continued..

As you can see shifting your mindset and leveraging systems is how everyone can make a fortune. Is it easy? Well, that depends on your skill level, commitment and work ethic. All I can say is it takes a lot of work and it's a process, and not overnight, and definitely not a get rich quick scheme.

So why the emphasis on online businesses? The scalability is massive and the entry point allows almost anyone with a internet connection to jump in on the bandwagon. The internet is a beautiful thing, literally connecting the world together, and expanding your horizons in regards to business. You can easily outsource work to cut costs, generate sales from outside your native land, and have layers and layers of protection encrypted by cyberspace. Over 3 billion people have access to the internet, with the internet you open up a global economy at the palm of your hands. - Imagine that all this from using a computer or laptop from home.

20-30 years ago you would need some serious funding to start any business venture, perhaps 100k. But if you opt for an online business you have very little start up costs and a low barrier entry point. Very low risk.

Net Worth

I'm sure you heard of the term "net worth" before? But what does it actually mean? Net worth is an evaluation of your current value after expenses. Essentially, gauging your total assets and your worth. Knowing your net worth and real value is actually a crucial component to business intelligence, and we'll soon see why.

You see there's a lot of people who claim to make millions or perhaps even six figures, but what is there actual net worth? It's very misleading to evaluate someone's value based on their generated revenue, and believe it or not a lot of people use this tactic to sell business plans, seminars and courses! It's not very honest or ethical to do so, and I'm going to show you how to find out one's true net worth and spot the deception.

For instance let's say John owns a drop shipping business and generates $10,000 in revenue a month. However, delivery fees, cost of production, storage fees, and marketing campings add up to $9,500 in total expenses. John's net worth after expenses would be valued at only ***$500***. How did we arrive at this conclusion? Please see my break down $10,000 revenue minus 9,500 expenses equates to a total of $500 net worth. So it would be very misleading of John to claim he makes 10k profit a month, which is not at all true!

Net worth reveals the true value of a person's business, and in this case John's drop shipping business is only worth $500, despite the substantial amount of revenue he generated. Therefore, remember this formula *Assets - Liabilities = net worth.* **(A-L = Net)**

The take home message here is not only to learn how to accurately determine one's net worth, but continually develop and accumulate assets that generate revenue, which in turn would increase your overall net worth.

Conclusion

Thank you for making it through to the end of *Data Analytics Guide: For Beginners Introduction*, let's hope it was informative and able to provide you with all of the tools you need to achieve your goals whatever it may be.

The next step is to take what you have learned here and begin to use it so that you can not only have better analysis when it comes to your data, but also so that you can make yourself valuable to your company that you are working for. Or, so that you can find a new job if that is what you are looking to do in order to advance in your goals.

Keep in mind that data analysis is not going to be easy and it is going to take a lot of time as well as patience for you to get the hang of it, but you are going to be able to do it. The important thing to remember is that there are going to be risks, but you should not allow those risks to stop you from doing your job. You are not only going to be making your job better, but you are going to be able to make other people's lives better.

Data analysis is in the world around us every day and we should not take it for granted due to the fact that what we see in the store is going to be there because of data that was gathered and analyzed to see if that product did good in the store or not. Not only that, but it also helps to improve products so that they are not in their first stages. Take a look at iPhone for example. There has been an iPhone released at least every other year with new features that the customer said they wanted on their phones. The same thing goes for when the phone updates. It is updating to improve applications and functions on the phone so that it runs better for their consumer. The same goes for the products that you find in the store. That is another reason why you can go to two different stores that are in the same franchise and find assorted products, it is not always demographics. It is based on the data that the company gets in what is bought in that community.

Hopefully thanks to this book, you are going to have a better understanding of data analytics and how it works in the world around you. If you picked up this book, it was obviously because you wanted to know more about data analysis so that you can change jobs or because you want to become better at the job that you already have. No matter what your reason is, good luck and thank you for picking up this book!

Finally, if you found this book useful in any way, a review on Amazon or on the site in which you purchased it is always appreciated!

Thank you and good luck!

If you enjoyed reading this book would you be kind enough to leave a quality review on Amazon? Thanks! Please see link below..